HOW SERMONS WORK

HOW
SERMONS
WORK

David Murray

PUBLISHING WITH A MISSION

EP BOOKS
Faverdale North, Darlington, DL3 0PH, England

e-mail: sales@epbooks.org
web: http://www.epbooks.org

EP BOOKS USA
P. O. Box 614, Carlisle, PA 17013, USA

e-mail: usasales@epbooks.org
web: http://www.epbooks.us

First published 2011

British Library Cataloguing in Publication Data available

ISBN-13: 978-085234-748-5
ISBN-10: 085234-748-0

Printed and bound in the USA by Versa Press Inc., East Peoria, IL.

Dedicated to my Dad and Mum.
Thanks for preaching and practising Christ.

ACKNOWLEDGEMENTS

I would like to thank David Woollin for inviting me to write for EP Books and also to Erroll Hulse for his advice and encouragement. Big thanks to Jackie Friston for her super-efficient editing and typesetting.

As you will soon see, I lean heavily on many past and present preachers both for my own formation and for training others to preach. In some ways, I'm teaching nothing original. However, I do hope that this book presents the accumulated wisdom of many gifted men in a clear, simple and useable way.

Finally, a very special thanks to Dr Joel Beeke for asking me to join him in team-teaching the preaching classes at Puritan Reformed Theological Seminary. There is no better teacher than teaching.

CONTENTS

INTRODUCTION

HOW DO THEY DO THAT?

One of my favourite childhood books was *How do they do that?* The Discovery Channel took the same idea and made it into a TV programme called *How do they do it?* The Internet has its own howstuffworks.com. These and other similar books, programmes, and web sites tap into our natural human curiosity. We want to know what lies behind the surface, what led up to the discovery, what makes what.

This book is a 'How do they do that?' about preaching. If it was a web site, we would call it howsermonswork.com. I've written it for four audiences. First, it is for seminary students who want a short practical guide on how to prepare and preach a sermon. They will read the classic books on preaching theory and practice as they continue their studies, but their 'practise preaching' class is looming and they desperately need a helping hand to get started. Here it is.

Second, the book is for elders. The material was originally prepared to help elders who were being asked to preach in various settings. I wanted to give these men a simple step-by-step guide to help them to prepare sermons in an efficient, enjoyable and edifying way. I've expanded the material since then to help more elders become more 'able to teach' (1 Tim. 3:2).

Third, I hope that even experienced preachers might pick up a crumb or two by reading this brief 'refresher'.

Fourth, although the book is about 'How sermons work', I've written it so that the vast majority of the material will be relevant and helpful to anyone who has to prepare a Bible message (e.g. for Sunday schools, Bible studies, etc.).

So it is not just for preachers. In fact, maybe above all I want non-preachers to read this book. Given that the most important hours in a Christian's week are the one or two hours they spend listening to their pastor's sermons, I find it surprising how few Christians are interested in 'How do they do that?'

Some people seem to think that pastors 'receive' their messages direct from God. They imagine some mysterious process by which the pastor just 'gets' a sermon. That is too high a view of preaching. It views preachers more like angels than ordinary mortals. I want to show that, just like any other work, there is a reasonable and logical method and system to follow.

Others think that a pastor just spends the week relaxing, gets up on a Sunday, and says the first thing that comes into his mind with little or no forethought or planning. That is too low a view of preaching. Anyone with a bit of verbal fluency could do it. I want to demonstrate that behind the thirty to forty-five minutes you see and hear on a Sunday morning are many hours of mental, spiritual and practical labour. Like all pastoral labour, it involves head, heart and hand.

If you want to increase respect for your pastor and his preaching, ask, 'How do they do that?' Then read this book and find out the answer.

1. PREPARATION

PREPARING TO PREACH

God prepares a man to preach the gospel by giving him certain convictions: convictions about his relationship to God, his relationship to his Bible, and his relationship to his people.

THE PREACHER AND HIS GOD

A preacher must have clear convictions about his relation to God.

A sinner saved by the grace of God

The pendulum of the preacher's heart must be continually swinging between two states. He must know that he is a hell-deserving sinner with a deceitful and desperately wicked heart. And he must know that he is saved by the grace of Jesus Christ through faith in his blood. The further and faster the pendulum swings between these two convictions, the better. No one has a right to preach who is not totally and utterly convinced of his own sinful misery and of Christ's saving mercy.

A sinner sent by the grace of God

Paul not only speaks of being saved by the grace of God, but also of being called and sent by the grace of God. 'To me, who am less than the least of all the saints, this grace was given, that I should preach among the Gentiles the unsearchable riches of Christ' (Eph. 3:8).

This is not the place to go into detail about the 'call to the ministry'. Suffice to say that the preacher should have two calls — the one internal and the other external. The exact nature of these calls varies from person to person. But, in general, we can say that the internal call is a burden or longing to preach based on right motives: the desires to obey God, to edify God's people, and to save souls. The external call is the church's confirmation of the internal call and involves the church's examination of the preacher's motives, gifts, character and Christian experience.

The preacher must work to maintain a constant sense of the divine call — when preparing to preach, when preaching, and when reflecting on the results of his preaching. This will set another pendulum swinging in his heart. It will swing from humility (resulting from the knowledge that it is divine mercy not human merit that has made him a preacher), to authority (resulting from the knowledge that God has commissioned him).

A sinner supplied with the gifts of God

Not only is the preacher saved by God's grace, and sent by God's grace, but he is also gifted by God's grace. A man can be gifted without being called and sent, but a man cannot be called and sent without being gifted. God supplies both the calling and the gifts to fulfil that calling.

What kind of gifts will be present in the preacher?

a. A strong self-discipline

As the preacher has no 'boss', no supervisor, or manager, he is able to do as little or as much as he desires, in whatever areas that interest him. Hence why so many lazy and undisciplined men have been attracted to the ministry. But when a man is truly called of God to the ministry, he is divinely equipped with an ability to organize and discipline himself to do his duty, even when there is no one to check up on him.

b. A love of studying

Paul admonished the young preacher, Timothy: 'Till I come, give attention to reading, to exhortation, to doctrine... Be diligent to present yourself approved to God, a worker who does not need to be ashamed, rightly dividing the word of truth' (1 Tim. 4:13; 2 Tim. 2:15). As the core of the preacher's task is the study of God's Word, God will usually bless the preacher with a love of studying.

c. An ability to communicate

As the preacher must not only understand the truth but also be able to communicate it clearly, God will usually give the preacher a clear mind and a clear voice, resulting in a clear message from God to men. God does not send messengers who confuse and bamboozle his people with displays of their learning — or their lack of it.

d. A love of people

There are many preachers who love their studies, but wish they never had to come out of them! They love preparing sermons, lectures and addresses, but seem to wish that they did not need a congregation to deliver them to. The God-sent messenger loves the people God has given to him. He enjoys visiting the flock and feeding the flock.

The gifts summarized above, and others, must be sought, cultivated, stirred up and developed (1 Tim. 4:14; 2 Tim. 1:6). J. W. Alexander warned:

> I fear none of us apprehend as we ought to do the value of the preacher's office. Our young men do not gird themselves for it with the spirit of those who are on the eve of a great conflict; nor do they prepare as those who are to lay their hands upon the springs of the mightiest passions, and stir up to their depths the ocean of human feelings.[1]

A sinner summoned to the bar of God

'Preach the word!' (2 Tim. 4:2) was Paul's last charge to Timothy and it was given in the context of the final judgement (v. 1). Paul's whole ministry was conducted in the awesome shadow of the last day. Knowing he would one day be called to give an account of his life and ministry he said, 'This being so, I myself always strive to have a conscience without offence toward God and men' (Acts 24:16). Al Martin writes:

> Next to the presence of Christ, there is no greater companion to the minister than that of a good conscience. To have the Lord at your side and a peaceful conscience in your breast — these are the preacher's two greatest companions.[2]

14

A constant awareness of the final judgement will help us to shun ignorance, dishonesty, laziness, vanity and self-seeking; and it will make us studious, honest, energetic, sober, prayerful and faithful.

SUMMARY

• If a preacher has clear convictions about who has saved, sent and supplied him, he will have a deep-seated and abiding humility before God.

• If a preacher knows that he is a divinely commissioned messenger, he will study with diligence and speak with clarity, authority and sobriety, knowing that one day he will be called to give an account to the one who sent him.

Princeton's James W. Alexander counselled a young preacher:

'My dear young friend, if there is anything you would rather be than a preacher of the gospel; if you regard it as a ladder to something else; if you do not consider all your powers as too little for the work; be assured you have no right to hope for any usefulness or even eminence.'[3]

THE PREACHER AND HIS BIBLE

God, in his mercy, has spoken and continues to speak to humanity through his works of creation and providence. While this 'general' revelation makes known God's goodness, wisdom and power, it is not enough to show a sinner the way of salvation. Consequently, in a further display of his mercy, God made a 'special' revelation of this necessary extra knowledge, to carefully chosen spokesmen, through theophanies, audible voices, dreams, visions, etc. The preacher must have certain clear convictions about this special revelation.

The inspiration of Scripture

First, he must believe that God, by a mighty work of the Holy Spirit, has infallibly secured an accurate and permanent written record of these special revelations in the Old and New Testaments. This work of the Holy Spirit, often called inspiration, secures an infallibility that extends to every word of Scripture, including those parts that make historical or scientific claims.

The authority of Scripture

In a day when Scripture is being questioned and undermined as never before, and when everyone regards his own opinion as authoritative, it is essential that the preacher be absolutely convinced of the ultimate authority of Scripture. The preacher must understand and communicate that the words he preaches are not his own but God's, and as such they are not optional but binding on all. Michael Barrett says that the Bible 'is the absolute standard of truth (matters of faith) and the absolute rule for living (matters of practice)'.[4] Like the Master, we must teach 'as one having authority, and not as the scribes' (Matt. 7:29).

The sufficiency of Scripture

The preacher must be convinced that the Word of God is God's all and only sufficient method of saving sinners and sanctifying saints (Heb. 4:12-13; Rom. 10:14ff). As the *Westminster Confession of Faith* puts it: 'The whole counsel of God, concerning all things necessary for his own glory, man's salvation, faith, and life, is either expressly set down in Scripture, or by good and necessary consequence may be deduced from Scripture: unto which nothing at any time is to be added, whether by new revelations of the Spirit, or traditions of men' (WCF 1.6).

The interpretation of Scripture[5]

Although there are difficult passages of Scripture, the preacher must be convinced that it can be interpreted by using the ordinary means God has provided. 'Those things which are necessary to be known, believed, and observed for salvation, are so clearly propounded, and opened in some place of Scripture or other, that not only the learned, but the unlearned, in a due use of the ordinary means, may attain unto a sufficient understanding of them' (WCF 1.7).

Michael Barrett finds the right balance here: 'God has made enough of His Word so crystal clear that only blind and blatant disbelief will not understand. He has made enough of His Word so deep that even the most faithful must depend on His enlightenment, rather than intellect.'[6]

SUMMARY

Clear and constant convictions regarding Scripture will motivate reading, study and enjoyment of it. A preacher must have a systematic plan of regularly reading through the whole Bible, with a portion from both the Old and New Testaments being read each day. Dedication and application are needed if he is to find the truths essential to faith and practice, as well as to his calling.

R. C. Sproul said, 'We fail in our duty to study God's Word not so much because it is difficult to understand, not so much because it is dull and boring, but because it is work. Our problem is not a lack of intelligence or a lack of passion. Our problem is that we are lazy.'

THE PREACHER AND HIS PEOPLE

The preacher must have convictions about his relationship to the people he is to preach to.

He is similar

The preacher must never imagine that he is better than his hearers. He may well be 'less than the least of all the saints' (Eph. 3:8). He is what he is by the grace of God — saved, sent and supplied by grace. The awareness that 'I am not better than them' will produce humility, sympathy, watchfulness, and a willingness to accept constructive criticism.

He is different

Though not by nature better than his hearers, the preacher must be different from his hearers. This is not an argument for aloofness and detachment. However, to whoever much is given, much shall be required (Luke 12:48); and much has been given to the preacher. He must be an example to his hearers and set higher standards than the norm.

Aristotle said that the secular orator must establish with his hearers a character for discretion (knowledge or judgement); second, for probity; and third, for benevolence, or good-will toward them. If this is true in the secular realm how much more in the sacred! R. L. Dabney challenges: 'Without a sacred weight of character, the most splendid rhetoric will win only a short-lived applause; with it, the plainest scriptural instructions are eloquent to win souls. Eloquence may dazzle and please; holiness of life convinces... The pastor's character speaks more loudly than his tongue.'[7]

SUMMARY

By holding the seeming paradox of similar yet different, the preacher will 'be an example to the believers, in word, in conduct, in love, in spirit, in faith, in purity' (1 Tim. 4:12), while maintaining a humble, approachable and sympathetic spirit.

2. SELECTION

SELECTING A TEXT

'What will I preach on?' That question challenges, vexes, and even haunts many preachers every day of their lives. Many answer the question by preaching on popular topics — social issues, politics, psychology, culture, etc. In fact J. I. Packer claims that, 'Topical preaching has become a general rule, at least in North America. Sermons explore announced themes rather than biblical passages.'[1] Packer gives the following reasons for this:

- To make preaching appear interesting and important in an age that has largely lost interest in the pulpit;
- To make the sermon sound different from what goes on in the Bible class before public worship starts;
- Many topical preachers (not all) do not trust their Bible enough to let it speak its own message through their lips.

He concludes:

Whatever the reason, however, the results are unhealthy. In a topical sermon the text is reduced to a peg on which the speaker hangs his line of thought; the shape and thrust of the message reflect his own best notions of what is good for people rather than being determined by the text itself... In my view topical discourses of this kind, no matter how biblical their component parts, cannot but fall short of being preaching in the full sense of that word, just because their biblical content is made to appear as part of the speaker's own wisdom... That destroys the very idea of Christian preaching, which excludes the thought of speaking for the Bible and insists that the Bible must be allowed to speak for itself in and through the speaker's words. Granted, topical discourses may become real preaching if the speaker settles down to letting this happen, but many topical preachers never discipline themselves to become mouthpieces for messages from biblical texts at all.[2]

I will qualify Packer's statement somewhat in the next chapter, when we look at topical preaching that is more theological than 'popular'. However, for the faithful gospel preacher, topical sermons will not be his staple diet. For him, the question is more limited than, 'What shall I preach on?' For him the question is, 'What portion of Scripture will I preach on?'

Although the preacher must preach the whole counsel of God, he cannot do this all in one sermon. Consequently, he must prepare separate addresses on separate portions of God's Word. Hence the question, 'What portion of Scripture or "text" will I preach on?'

We will consider three questions in this chapter: (1) What is a text?; (2) Why choose a text?; (3) How to choose a text?

WHAT IS A TEXT?

Definition of 'text'

The word 'text' is from the Latin *textum*, meaning woven. This suggests that as the sermon 'text' is woven into the whole fabric of the Scriptures, it must not be torn out of its connections and relations with the rest of Scripture. It also indicates that the 'text' must be woven into the whole fabric of the sermon. The 'text' must be taken from Scripture, be shown in its relation to the rest of Scripture, and be the substance of the sermon.

Defining a 'text'

How much Scripture constitutes a 'text'? Can a text be one word or one phrase? Must it be one whole verse? May it extend to many verses? The best way to answer these questions is to consider the three main kinds of 'texts'.

a. Single verse texts

These texts contain the cardinal truths of redemption: original sin, new birth, justification, the deity of Christ, etc. Although they will be set in their scriptural context the majority of the sermon is focused on the exposition of one verse. The text should not be simply a motto to introduce the sermon, but should regulate the whole sermon.

Example: 'The soul who sins shall die' (Ezek. 18:20). A sermon on such a text will explain what sin is, what death is, and how they are connected. But it will also show the connection with Ezekiel's previous line of argument, and also its relation to the doctrines of sin and death in other parts of Scripture.

b. Conclusion texts

This might be one phrase or one sentence that gives the moral of a whole parable, or the summary of the whole passage. However, the preacher must also expound the connected passage that leads up to the 'conclusion'.

Example: 'And I say to you, make friends for yourselves by unrighteous mammon, that when you fail, they may receive you into an everlasting home' (Luke 16:9). This is a summary of the parable in verses 1-8 and any sermon should explain both the parable and the summary.

c. Multiple verse texts

Such texts involve the exposition of two or more verses at a time. The text's start and finish points will be determined by a number of factors — the genre of the literature (historical narrative, doctrine, poetry, etc.), the density of the material (doctrinal, devotional, etc.), the variety of subjects (where a new subject is introduced or a new argument is begun), the length of time available for the sermon, etc.

Multiple-verse texts are often part of a series of consecutive sermons through a chapter or a whole book. There are advantages to this method:

- The pastor and congregation are 'stretched' to preach on and hear about subjects that would not be normally chosen;
- The preacher and hearers are immersed in the book for many weeks;

- It helps to keep passages in context;
- It teaches people how to read and study their Bibles;
- It provides a balanced diet and prevents pastors from sticking to their 'hobby horses';
- The pastor does not need to agonize over his choice of text each week;
- There does not need to be so much introduction and background given each week;
- The overall argument or narrative of the book is better grasped and understood;
- It helps people to see the overall plan of Scripture;
- It encourages people to prepare ahead by reading and thinking about the passage;
- It emphasizes the centrality and authority of Scripture.

But having stated the advantages, let me also advise how to avoid the disadvantages.

- While using the criteria mentioned above for deciding the start and finish points, special care should be taken to ensure that each sermon is complete in itself;
- The portion of Scripture chosen should not be too few verses, so that the series goes on too long, or too many, so that the preaching becomes shallow and superficial;
- There should be a memorable theme and points for each sermon rather than making it a running commentary;
- It may be helpful to read a related passage of Scripture rather than the same portion every week for many weeks;
- The need for variation should be prayerfully considered. For example, a series on a Pauline Epistle might be followed by a Gospel or an Old Testament narrative book;
- There should be a break in the series from time to time to provide a change. Sometimes it may be wise to take a break for a few weeks or even months before returning to it;

- A pastor should be prepared to preach on a text the Lord 'lays on his heart' even if it breaks the sermon series;
- Preachers should be conscious of their limitations. Few preachers can sustain their congregation's interest in a long series of consecutive expository sermons, especially if two or more series are going on at the same time;
- Before finally deciding to start a series, the preacher should read the book through a few times and begin to map out preaching portions. This will also help him to decide if this is the right book and if his own gifts will stretch enough to take it on;
- As this is a major decision that will set the course of the congregation for a while, it may be wise to consult with some carefully chosen elders or mature Christians;
- He must avoid the danger of becoming a mere teacher or lecturer rather than a preacher;
- He should remember to preach evangelistically, not just to the Christians in the congregation;
- There is no need for a long recap at the beginning of every sermon.

Example: Genesis 6:1-10 would be a suitable portion for consecutive exposition. Its beginning and ending are clearly marked. It begins with a horrendous description of the state of the earth in the days of Noah, and God's displeasure. It ends with the holy description of Noah walking with God, and God's delight in him.

John Stott explains how although the length of text may vary, what we do with it remains the same:

> The size of the text is immaterial, so long as it is biblical. What matters is what we do with it. Whether it is long or short, our responsibility as expositors is to open it up in such a way that it speaks its message clearly, plainly, accurately, relevantly without addition, subtraction or

falsification. In expository preaching the biblical text is neither a conventional introduction to a sermon on a largely different theme, nor a convenient peg on which to hang a ragbag of miscellaneous thoughts, but a master which dictates and controls what is said.[3]

SUMMARY

The text should be a portion of Scripture that is explained in relation to its context. Care should be taken to define the limits of the text, explain the text, and show its relations to its context and the rest of Scripture. All preaching should be expository in substance, however long the text may be.

WHY CHOOSE A TEXT?

Let us now consider six advantages of choosing a text of Scripture as the basis for exposition in a sermon.

First, this is the scriptural practice in both the Old Testament (Neh. 8:5-8) and the New Testament (Luke 4:16-19; Acts 2:14-36).

Second, it honours Scripture. It clearly communicates that the Bible is our only rule of faith and practice.

Third, it distinguishes the sermon from merely human words, and insofar as the sermon explains God's Word it possesses divine authority. Dabney said, 'The whole authority of his addresses to the conscience depends upon the correspondence between his explanations and inferences and the infallible word.'[4]

Similarly, the *Westminster Directory of Public Worship* says,

In raising doctrines from the text, his care ought to be, *First,* That the matter be the truth of God. *Secondly,* That it be a truth contained in or grounded on that text, that the hearers may discern how God teacheth it from thence.

Thirdly, That he chiefly insist upon those doctrines which are principally intended; and make most for the edification of the hearers.

Fourth, it tethers the preacher to the Scriptures, ensuring that they are explained in public and, therefore, that God is revealed to the public.

Fifth, text-based sermons are more likely to have structure and unity, making them more easily remembered by both the preacher and the hearers.

Sixth, the wide variety of texts in the Scriptures is more likely to produce variety in exposition and interest in the hearers.

Seventh, it sets limits. Donald Coggan called this 'the magnificent tyranny of the Gospel!' He said,

> The Christian preacher has a boundary set for him. When he enters the pulpit, he is not an entirely free man. There is a very real sense in which it may be said of him that the Almighty has set him his bounds that he shall not pass. He is not at liberty to invent or choose his message: it has been committed to him, and it is for him to declare, expound and commend it to his hearers... It is a great thing to come under the magnificent tyranny of the Gospel![5]

SUMMARY

Sermons that explain the text of Scripture conform to the scriptural example, honour the Scriptures, communicate authority, reveal God, and help listeners to listen and remember.

HOW TO CHOOSE A TEXT

Having established what is a text and highlighted the advantages of preaching from a text, we shall now look at helps to choosing a text. This is perhaps the most important task in any preacher's life. It is also often the most problematic. W. G. T. Shedd then Charles Spurgeon explain:

> The greatest possible labour and care should be expended upon the choice of a text... As in secular oratory, the selection of a subject is either vital or fatal to the whole performance. So in sacred oratory, the success of the preacher depends entirely upon the fitness of his choice of a text... Labour at this point saves labour at all after points.[6]

> I hope we all make it a matter of very earnest and serious consideration, every week, what shall be the subjects upon which we shall address our people on the Sabbath morning and evening; for, although all Scripture is good and profitable, yet it is not all equally appropriate for every occasion.[7]

We shall consider the source of texts, and the substance of texts.

The source of texts

a. Read the Bible

The preacher should be reading his Bible primarily to edify his own soul. But, in the ordinary course of this reading, he will come across suitable sermon texts that grip him, move him and interest him.

b. Read good books

As time for reading is limited, the preacher should make sure he is reading the books that will produce the most sermons. By that

I do not mean the reading of books of sermons, but books that will refer to Scripture, explain Scripture, and highlight Scripture in a way that may form the basis of a sermon.

c. Listen to people

In the course of pastoral visitation, subjects will arise that will stimulate the mind and suggest texts for sermons. Sinclair Ferguson speaks of bringing two horizons together in selecting a text:

> Our first principle must be to recognize (whether we preach from a single section, or through an entire book of the Bible) that the preacher operates with two horizons: (1) the text of Scripture and (2) the people of God and their environment in the world. He ought not normally to make his selection without consciously bringing these two horizons together.[8]

Some have had a 'Sermon Suggestion Box' or have invited regular reviews and previews of sermons with their elders in order to re-balance, plan, etc.

d. Read/watch/listen to the news

I do not intend to suggest here that news headlines become sermon texts. However, the daily news will highlight trends in thought, in religion, in lifestyle and in morals that the pastor may want to address from a biblical perspective.

e. Observe providence

Momentous events like war, earthquakes, disease and tragedies will often supply a relevant introduction to a sermon, say, on

God's providence and our response to it. God's people will often go to church with questions about national and world events. They may be wondering: 'Is there a word from the Lord on this?'

f. Consider available resources

Some pastors may have very limited money to buy commentaries. In such circumstances, rather than trying to buy a commentary on each and every book of the Bible, it may be better to buy a number of commentaries on one book of the Bible and preach their way through that book over a period of time. The lack of resources may be part of God's guidance on what to preach!

g. Listen to God

It may seem strange to put this after these other sources, as the sources just mentioned are all ways in which we listen to God. However, what I am referring to here specifically is the necessity of the preacher to remain sensitive to the voice of God in his own soul. God, who searches all spirits, will at times directly impress a text upon the spirit of the preacher. The preacher may not know the reason for this, but should respond to it, trusting that God has seen a need, invisible perhaps to everyone else, and knows the text to address it. J. W. Alexander describes it like this:

> The right text is the one which comes of itself during reading and meditation: which accompanies you in walks, goes to bed with you, and rises with you. On such a text thoughts swarm and cluster, like bees upon a branch.[9]

Charles Spurgeon takes us further than simply listening to God for a text. He urges that we cry to God for it:

When your text comes in answer to prayer, it will be all the dearer to you; it will come with a divine savour and unction altogether unknown to the formal orator.[10]

Such 'personal' texts have been called 'luminous' or 'phosphorescent' texts. Campbell Morgan tells how he was in Dr Joseph Parker's vestry at the City Temple one day when a man came in and said to him, 'I want to thank you for that sermon. It did me good.' Dr Parker looked at him and replied: 'Sir, I preached it because it had done me good.'

It is important to mention here that preachers must not limit themselves to verses that they have personally 'experienced'. For example, they have to preach on marriage even if they are unmarried. They have to preach on dealing with doubt and spiritual darkness even if they have had no troubles with this.

SUMMARY

If the preacher has read his Bible, kept his mind refreshed with good books, visited people, stayed abreast of current affairs, observed providence, and remained sensitive to God's voice, the problem will not be a lack of 'texts' but an embarrassment of riches. In order to preserve these riches in store for future use, preachers should keep a pocket notebook in which to write 'texts' sourced in these ways, together with 'skeletons' of sermons.

The substance of texts

Having considered some possible sources of texts, let us now think about the substance of texts. What are the characteristics of appropriate texts?

a. Complete

However long or short, the text should be complete. It should not be a mere fragment of Scripture nor a piece of Scripture used as a motto. The markers for where a text begins and ends have already been discussed above and will be further examined in the chapter on exegesis.

b. Important

The text must contain an important point. While every verse in Scripture is important, not all contain important truths. Many connect those that do. The Holy Spirit did not intend a sermon in every sentence of Scripture. We must therefore major on the majors.

c. Brief

While aiming for a 'complete' text, the preacher should also consider that briefer texts are more memorable than long texts. If preaching from a multiple-verse text, a preacher may summarize the whole passage before limiting himself to one particularly striking verse in it.

d. Clear

The plainer the text is the better. If there is a choice of texts to teach one truth, then the simplest one should usually be chosen and used to cast light on the more complex.

Shedd said,

> The text is the key-note to the whole sermon ... The more bold, the more undoubted and undisputed its tone, the better... It challenges attention and gets it. It startles and

impresses by its direct and authoritative announcement of a great and solemn proposition. Nothing remains, then, but for the preacher to go out upon it with his whole weight, to unfold and apply its evident undoubted meaning, with all the moral confidence and all the serious earnestness of which he is capable.[11]

e. Natural

A sermon should not be forced into a text but should be derived from it in a plain, natural and obvious manner. Avoid oddity and eccentricity. The apostle argues for things that 'are good and profitable to men' and against curiosity, speculation and the things that are 'unprofitable and useless' (2 Tim. 2:15, 16, 23; Titus 3:8-9).

f. Varied

We will deal with how to vary sermons in chapter 4, but the preaching calendar should be reviewed to ensure the right balance between Old and New Testament, the wrath of God and love of God, narrative and doctrine, etc. Only balanced preaching will leave the impression God intended with the mould of Scripture. Imbalanced preaching will distort the mould and its impression on the hearers.

g. Suitable

The selection of texts may be influenced by the time of year (harvest, Communion, war, etc.). Selection may also be influenced by the spiritual needs of the congregation: what sins they are falling into, what joys they celebrate, what trials they are facing, etc. Sinclair Ferguson explains:

But alongside this objective exercise, there is an exercise in spiritual sensitivity also required in the selection of preaching material. The preacher is not a systematic theologian whose exclusive task is to expound an inwardly coherent account of the Christian faith. He is a pastor, whose major task is to feed the flock of God. The context of the congregation therefore plays a major role in the selection of his material. Where are they in terms of the Christian pilgrimage? What are their situations, needs, lacks, pressures, composition? Of course our preaching is not to be *need-determined,* but it must be *people-oriented,* as Jesus Christ's was (cf. John 16:12).[12]

Spurgeon said we must pick the food suited to the hearers.

We dare not rush into the King's banquet hall with a confusion of provisions as though the entertainment were to be a vulgar scramble, but as well-mannered servitors we pause and ask the great Master of the feast, Lord, what wouldst thou have us set upon thy table this day?[13]

SUMMARY

- When selecting the text, the preacher should ask: 'Is it complete, is it important, is it brief, is it clear, is it natural, is it varied, and is it suitable?'

Dabney cautions: 'I would impress you with a solemn awe of taking any liberties in expounding the word. I would have you feel that every meaning of the text, other than that which God expressly intended it to bear, is forbidden fruit to you, however plausible and attractive — fruit which you dare not touch on peril of a fearful sin.'[14]

3. INTERROGATION

EXEGETING THE TEXT

Exegesis is the process that is used to explain the meaning and message of a text of Scripture. In this chapter we will lay a foundation for approaching the exegetical task, and then list a number of questions to help us build our exegesis in a structured and systematic way.

EXEGETICAL FOUNDATIONS

Before we begin the process of exegesis, let us be sure that we understand the following.

Exegesis begins with prayer

Prayerless exegesis is possible, but not profitable for the exegete or his hearers. Prayerful exegesis honours God, blesses the exegete, and is much more likely to discover truth and meaning than mere natural reasoning and logic.

Exegesis is hard work

If anyone does not agree with that statement now, I hope they will by the end of this chapter. Once they see the amount of mental discipline and rigour required to interpret the Bible correctly, they will perhaps rather carry bricks or dig holes all day!

Sometimes the exegete may have to rip up hours of labour (or press the delete key) when he realizes that his initial interpretation was all wrong. Dr Martyn Lloyd-Jones said that a preacher must 'sacrifice a good sermon rather than force a text'. Usually, of course, the results are worth the effort, but getting there can involve a lot of dull, monotonous and exhausting hours.

The human mind will often prefer to do anything but this. It is so much easier to write emails, make phone calls, read good books, etc. That is why the preacher must carve out lengthy and concentrated periods of study to exegete a passage of Scripture aright. Exegesis will never succeed by grabbing fifteen minutes of study here and there. Neither can much be accomplished with the baby playing in the study, the radio on, and email open! The exegete needs prolonged time and undistracted quiet.

Jay Adams believed that the root cause of so much bad preaching today is the lack of hard work.

> My point is that good preaching demands hard work. From listening to sermons and from talking to hundreds of preachers about preaching, I am convinced that the basic reason for poor preaching is the failure to spend adequate time and energy in preparation. Many preachers — perhaps most — simply don't work long enough on their sermons.[1]

W. E. Sangster wrote of how the preacher must labour at 'sheer thinking: assembling the facts, facing their apparent contradiction, reaching up for the help of God and, then, driving his brain like a bulldozer through the apparent chaos to order and understanding at the last'.[2]

Exegesis can be learned

If exegesis is some mystical experience that only a select few find the magic key to, then most preachers are left to helpless despair. But if a large part of the process is hard work, then that gives everyone hope. Of course, some are more gifted at exegesis than others. However, if a man is called of God and gifted by the Holy Spirit then he can learn how to exegete a passage of Scripture. The approach will vary a bit depending on the kind of passage being considered, and each preacher's temperament, gifts and situation will also play a part, but most exegetical skills can be learned.

Exegesis gets easier

Like everything in life, practice makes perfect — especially if good practices are learned early and followed in a disciplined way. With practice, the exegetical process becomes part of the preacher's psyche. He sees a text, his mind instinctively follows the good habits he has learned, and eventually he will find texts opening up to him, dividing themselves before his very eyes, suggesting applications, etc. Sometimes he will think, 'Why did I ever think this was so hard?'

Exegesis is practical

I wholeheartedly agree with Douglas Stuart that exegesis should be guided by practical considerations.

Exegesis is patently a theological enterprise, and a theology that is not applied to the lives of God's people is sterile... The end of exegesis is preaching and teaching in the church. Seminary students and pastors know this instinctively and demand relevance from exegesis and other biblical studies, as well they should.[3]

Stuart believes that critical techniques of exegesis should be used 'only insofar as these, too, hold promise of practical theological benefit.'

The results [of exegesis] should always at least be of genuine practical value to this believer, or something is wrong with the exegesis.[4]

The preacher should, however, keep in view that the overall purpose of the Bible is to make a person wise unto salvation through faith in Jesus Christ (2 Tim. 3:15).

He should also remember that God promises more light and understanding to those who believe and obey his Word (James 1:22-25; 2 Peter 1:5-8; 1 Peter 3:7).

Exegesis must be limited

There is virtually no limit to the amount of time that can be spent or the number of resources that can be consulted in exegeting a text of Scripture. In seminary a student might spend between fifteen and twenty hours on an exegetical paper. In pastoral ministry, time is much more limited — maybe more like eight to ten hours. Exegesis, therefore, must focus on the areas of exegesis that will yield the most benefit in the least amount of time.

Exegesis asks questions

The exegete does not come to his text with answers but with questions. There are primarily two questions to ask: 'What did the text mean?' and 'What does the text say?' These two central questions about a text's meaning and message are answered by asking the text a number of other questions, and it is these questions we will study in this chapter.

Exegesis is not preaching

Exegesis is not the finished product but rather a servant to it. It is not the end of the road but the road to the end — the preached sermon. The pulpit is the place for preaching a sermon not for sharing our exegetical homework. Robert Thomas says,

> Very few in the pew have a background sufficient to enable them to comprehend the kind of technical data derived from exegesis. So the minister of the Word must adapt his explanations to suit the vocabulary and interest level of those to whom he speaks. He must develop a technique of conveying in the language of a non-specialist what he has learned from his specialized analysis. How he does so may vary. It may be through paraphrase, description, analogy, illustration, or in a multitude of other ways. Yet he must explain the text in a way that is interesting and understandable to his people. This explanation is the core of Bible exposition.[5]

EXEGETICAL QUESTIONS

As the preacher prepares his heart and mind for prayerful interrogation of the text, there are some questions he can consider which will open up the text and yield its meaning. There are five main types of questions.

A. Translation questions
B. Background questions
C. Textual questions
D. Contextual questions
E. Final questions

Translation questions

1. What are the limits of the text?

In chapter two, we touched on the nature of a text and how to find its beginning and end points. These guidelines can be used to ensure that the text is complete. Paragraph markers include time, place and character changes in narratives. In poetic literature, genre and mood shifts can be helpful identifiers. In more doctrinal passages words like, 'so', 'therefore', 'now', can highlight transitions.

Although our chapter and verse divisions are not in the original text of Scripture, it can be helpful to check if the preaching passage matches the paragraphing of our English Bible.

2. Which translation?

Any knowledge of Hebrew and Greek will assist in translating the passage of Scripture. Parsing guides and lexicons, in paper or electronic form, can also give a helping hand. Trying to think of alternative words to those in our usual Bible version will also be edifying. Jogging the mind out of its familiar 'ruts' can open up new avenues of thought. Any alternative translations and important words should be written down for further study.

3. What do the lexicons say?

Using a lexicon to read articles on the important words selected in step 2 is particularly helpful. Lexicons list the possible meanings that a word can have in differing situations, and will offer opinions about the right meaning in this particular context.

4. What are the tenses, moods and voices of the verbs?

The verbs should be parsed in order to find out their tense, mood and voice. In Greek there may be significance in the use of an aorist tense over against a perfect tense. In Hebrew there may be significance in the use of a participle rather than a perfect tense, a Piel rather than a Qal.

5. What syntactical features are important?

Syntax is concerned with the way words are joined in sentences and paragraphs. The order of the words may reveal an emphasis intended by the author. Is there an imperative followed by a number of participles?

Example: When Paul commands believers to be filled with the Spirit in Ephesians 5:18, he goes on to define that imperative with five participles (-ing words). In other words, the people who are filled with the Spirit will demonstrate it in these five companion virtues.

6. How do other versions translate the text?

Having made the translation and become familiar with the text in the original language, various English translations should then be consulted. I use the KJV, NKJV, NIV, ESV, NASB, YLT,

GNB, and The Message. Some of these are more paraphrases than translations. However, I have often found that they provide good sermon material, or good language for explaining the text due to their being more interpretations than translations. Any personal translation should be checked against credible established versions and any necessary corrections, expansions, or contractions made.

Example: Notice the extra light which the NKJV throws on the underlined phrase below.

'For thou <u>preventest him</u> with the blessings of goodness: thou settest a crown of pure gold on his head'
(Ps. 21:3, KJV).

'For You <u>meet him</u> with the blessings of goodness; You set a crown of pure gold upon his head'
(Ps. 21:3, NKJV).

There is much to be said for doing this work early in the week and regularly meditating on the verse in its original language and in translation.

Even without Greek or Hebrew, much of this work can still be done by using Bible software like Logos or Bible Works, or by using the online NET Bible.

Background questions

1. Is the text in the Old Testament or the New Testament?

This is an important question to ask, because the meaning of words and concepts may vary depending on whether the text is under the 'Old Covenant' or under the 'New Covenant' dispensation.

There are a few pitfalls to avoid here. First, the temptation to interpret the Old Testament as if the original writer and readers had the light of the New Testament should be resisted. It is very important to first ask what the original writer and reader understood with the light they enjoyed. Second, there is a danger of getting 'stuck' in the Old Testament. Some scholars are so fearful of leap-frogging the original meaning that they never get past it. Jesus warrants the use of New Testament light to further interpret Old Testament passages (Luke 24:25-27).

Example: The ceremonial laws requiring various sacrifices under the 'Old Covenant' have been abolished by the final and full sacrifice of Jesus Christ under the 'New Covenant'. Any sermon on these laws would have to explain what they originally meant to the original audience. How did they understand and use these verses? But we must not stop there. We must go on to show how the New Testament has abolished these sacrifices, while giving them continued theological significance.

2. What book does the verse appear in?

If the previous question will help place the text in its covenantal context, this question will help set it in its canonical context. By identifying the book's place in God's progressive revelation of himself, we will more safely arrive at its original meaning and avoid importing later revelations of God into our interpretation.

Example: While God's use of the plural 'let us make' in Genesis 1 allows for the later doctrine of the Trinity, it is not certain that the original readers interpreted this as a plurality of persons in the Godhead. The revelation of God as one in three persons was progressively and increasingly revealed as the canon of Scripture unfolded.

3. What is the historical background?

By identifying when the events of the text took place, we can find other passages of Scripture that refer to that time, and any significant links to events that came before or after. It is important to work on educating hearers in biblical chronology.

In connection with this, Douglas Stuart wrote:

> Most churchgoers know few dates. They usually aren't sure whether Esther comes before or after Abraham, or in what century to locate any of them. The more often you take the time to explain the dates related to a passage (it need not take very long, after all), the more clear the interrelationships of people, books, and events will become to your congregation. God's revelation to us is a historical one — do not neglect chronology.[6]

It is very difficult for people to remember dates. I would suggest painting with a broad brush to give people a sense of the order of events. Although some accuracy is sacrificed, that can come later when the general order of biblical history has crystallized in their minds. Here are the principal historical pillars of biblical history.

BC

4000 Primeval Age: Creation, Fall, Flood, Babel
2000 Patriarchal Age: Abraham, Isaac, Jacob, Joseph
1500 Mosaic Age: Moses, Joshua
1000 Davidic Age; David, Solomon
700   Israel exiled to Assyria
600   Judah exiled to Babylon
500   Restoration: Ezra, Nehemiah

AD

30   Christ's ministry & death

70   Romans destroy Jerusalem

Example: Further light can be shed on Ezra and Nehemiah by studying the prophets Haggai, Zechariah and Malachi, who also ministered just before and during that time.

Sometimes, it is not possible to say for certain when events took place. However, we might carefully suggest appropriate life settings. This might be done with some of the untitled Psalms.

4. What is the geographical setting?

Where did the events take place? In or outside Israel, in the north or the south, in a city or in a home, etc.? Listeners are helped to paint the scene in their minds if preachers are able to describe the relative locations of places or the terrain of the setting.

Douglas Stuart commented:

> Many preachers report that the results of this part of the process especially produce the sorts of remarks in a sermon that cause members of a congregation to say that they felt like they were 'right there', i.e., able to imagine themselves in something of the same relationship to the biblical material that the original audience presumably was.[7]

Example: The humanly impossible situation Israel faced at the Red Sea is emphasized by describing the geographical cul-de-sac of mountains, desert, sea and Egyptians on each side.

5. Who is the author?

Sometimes this is stated. However, even if we cannot be 100% sure of the author, his character is sometimes evident. Douglas Stuart wrote:

> To a listener, a passage of Scripture often seems more 'real' if its author has been identified and the general character of his writing has been described just a bit.[8]

Example: When preaching from the Psalms written by David, it is helpful to try and relate the sentiments in the Psalm to David's character and life.

6. When was it written?

This may have been many years after the events narrated took place. Knowing who wrote, when he wrote, and to whom he wrote might help us to understand what and why he wrote.

Example: Genesis was written by Moses, which means that it was written many years after the events narrated in the book. It appears that Moses was using Israel's ancient history to guide the nation regarding its present duty to leave Egypt behind and press on into the promised land.

7. To whom was it written?

When trying to discover the original meaning of a text, it is vital to ask, 'To whom was the text originally written?' We have to travel back in time and sit with the original hearers and readers to understand what needs were being addressed. Sidney Greidanus says,

A major reason for seeking the purpose of the author is, therefore, consciously to shift attention away from ourselves to the Scriptures, away from our concerns to the author's concerns, away from our own purposes to the author's purpose. In other words, asking for the author's purpose is an attempt at genuine listening by cutting out all subjective interference.[9]

8. What kind of literature is it?

A full treatment of the way that genre affects interpretation deserves a separate volume, but let me briefly note here some of the areas to watch out for in interpreting the different genres of biblical literature. Different literary categories are prose, song, wisdom, apocalyptic, biography, narrative, prophecy, legal code, etc. The preacher will gradually develop a feel for the different approaches required for different genres of Scripture.

Examples

When preaching from Daniel, the historical narrative sections will be interpreted quite differently from the apocalyptic, or visionary parts. While both sections communicate reality and truth, the former will be interpreted literally and the latter figuratively. Much of Ezekiel and Revelation also come under the category of apocalyptic.

Devotional material like the Psalms will usually have less exposition and more application than, say, a text from Ephesians chapter 1.

When preaching from wisdom literature, care must be taken to balance the practical wisdom of the Proverbs and some of the Psalms, with the more philosophical wisdom found in Job and Ecclesiastes. Practical wisdom gives general principles that commonly operate in an ideal world. Philosophical wisdom recognizes that we live in a less-than-ideal world in which common general principles are sometimes, in God's providence, turned upside down.

Sometimes the message of a book is much more subtle than we would expect. For example, the general tenor of Ecclesiastes seems very pessimistic. However, it would be a mistake to interpret it as just a pessimistic look at this world (life under the sun). There are thirteen brief optimistic passages scattered throughout the book that describe another way of living, a way of living 'above the sun', a way of living with God in the picture (e.g. Eccles. 2:24-26; 3:12-15; 5:18-20; 8:15). The last chapter concludes on this hopeful note too.

Many today interpret the Song of Solomon as a simple narrative about human love. However, while some past commentators have seen a measure of historical narration in the story, most of them have also seen the song as symbolic of the love between God and Israel, or between Christ and his Church.

Prophecies may have immediate fulfilment and more distant fulfilments. For example, the numerous predictions of a rebuilt temple in Ezekiel were partially fulfilled after Israel's return from Babylonian exile around 538 BC. But it was further fulfilled in the coming of Christ as God's temple (John, 2:19-21), continues to be fulfilled in the building of Christ's church in and through his people (1 Cor. 6:19; 1 Peter 2:5), and will be finally fulfilled in the new heavens and new earth (Rev. 21). We can call this the '3 Cs of prophecy-fulfilment': commencement, continuation and consummation.

When preaching from parables, the immediate context will often help identify the main lesson or point of the parable, and prevent allegorizing.

Narrative preaching, especially Old Testament narrative preaching, has the tendency to become merely moralistic and exemplary. Hebrews 11 helps us to interpret many of these passages in a Christocentric way, by showing that it was faith in the Messiah that motivated the words and actions of Bible personalities. Also, each narrative must be seen as a link in an unbroken chain of redemptive history. In every narrative we trace conflict to the promise of Genesis 3:15 and the resolution to the fulfilment at Calvary and, ultimately, the new heavens and the new earth.

Doctrinal texts will require more close and detailed analysis of words, grammar and syntax, whereas narrative portions often require the preacher to 'step back' more from the text in order to discern the meaning and message in the bigger picture.

Textual questions

1. What are the main words in the text?

It is useful to list all the important verbs, nouns and adjectives. This will not only help when performing word studies, but maybe also in structuring the sermon. Particular attention should be given as to whether any words are used repeatedly.

Example: "'In those days and in that time,' says the LORD, "The children of Israel shall <u>come</u>, they and the children of Judah together; with continual <u>weeping</u> they shall <u>come</u>, and <u>seek</u> the LORD their God'" (Jer. 50:4). The key verbs here are underlined and may also provide sermon headings.

2. What are the most important places or personalities?

This can prove a suitable source of further research in Bible encyclopaedias and also of potential sermon headings.

Example: A sermon on Genesis 16 might look at events from four different perspectives based on the main personalities: Abram, Sarai, Hagar and Ishmael.

3. What doctrines are involved?

Explicit or implicit doctrines in the text should be highlighted for further study.

Example: 'And he [Abraham] believed in the LORD, and He accounted it to him for righteousness' (Gen. 15:6). This verse would require the consideration of the doctrine of justification by faith and imputed righteousness.

4. What is central and what is peripheral?

Preachers should learn to distinguish between what is of primary and what is of secondary importance in a text. It is not possible to say everything about every text in every sermon. Nor is it necessary. It is better to major on the majors and minor on the minors, and to remember what is the main message in each passage.

Example: When preaching on the Red Sea crossing, it is best to not get diverted by all the speculation about what and where the Red Sea actually was. The most important point is the divine miracle of the crossing.

5. How is the text structured?

This is especially relevant when looking at more than one verse. Is there a logical structure (e.g. a syllogism), a chronological structure (beginning, middle and end), an emotional structure (moving from despair to hope), a parallel structure (same thing said twice), etc.

Example: Many Psalms move from despair to hope. Many Proverbs say the same thing twice, though in different ways.

Contextual questions

1. How is the text connected with the surrounding verses, chapters, or even books?

Certain connecting words such as 'and, therefore, however, but, nevertheless, then, etc.' should be noted particularly.

Example: The connections between the various books of the Pentateuch are notable. Also, the Ten Commandments are preceded with a statement of redemption (Exod. 20:2), and concluded with a reference to sacrifice. Making these connections will help to prevent legalistic sermons on the commandments.

2. Is there selectivity?

Some books repeat what is told in other books. However, they usually present the same events in a different way. The writer is inspired to select the facts which will best serve his overall purpose. By understanding this selectivity we can gain clues to the overall purpose of the writer.

Example: The books of Kings and Chronicles cover many of the same events. However, Kings was written before the Babylonian captivity and highlights the sins of the kings that caused the captivity. Chronicles was written after the nation had been taken captive to Babylon and presents the line of David in a more positive light in order to re-kindle hope of a restoration of the Davidic kingdom and the Messianic hope.

3. Are there any cultural references?

By identifying practices unique to Israelite culture we can avoid illegitimate transfers of culturally specific practices. A Bible dictionary or encyclopaedia can help in discerning whether certain practices were culturally bound only to the state of Israel. Some may have a transferable principle, though no longer literally practised.

Example: The necessity of building a fence around the roof of one's home was only relevant to a flat-roofed culture in which the roof was often used for practical and social purposes. However, it is worth pointing out that there is a transferable principle of taking responsibility for others' safety while on our property which is not culturally bound.

4. Are there any cross-references?

Is the text quoted, alluded to, interpreted or developed in other parts of Scripture? A thorough cross-reference resource like the *Thomson Chain Reference Bible,* or the *New Treasury of Scripture Knowledge* will be of help here. Such resources are not only useful for seeing how Old Testament truths are fulfilled in the New, but also for seeing how Old Testament truths form the basis for so many New Testament concepts.

Example: Genesis 16:6 is referred to in Romans 4; Galatians 3; and James 2.

Final questions

Under this heading I want to highlight a few other questions that do not fit neatly under any of the previous categories. But although I say that these are final questions, I do not mean that they are always the last questions. I like to view exegesis more as a spiral than as a step-by-step process. In other words, exegetical steps are not to be followed A-B-C...Z, etc., but A-B-C, then A-B-C-D-E-F, then A-B, etc. We keep revising earlier conclusions in the light of later research. We spiral downwards rather than skim forwards.

My four final questions are in the realms of Christology, application, disagreement and commentaries.

1. Where is the Christology?

A sermon that fails to preach Christ has failed. It is hard to fail like that when preaching from the New Testament, but it is much easier to fail at this when preaching from the Old Testament. Here are some helps.

a. Prophecies

One of the easiest ways to preach Christ from the Old Testament is to preach the prophecies that were fulfilled, either explicitly or implicitly in his person and work.

b. Pictures

The person and work of Christ are also presented in Old Testament passages by way of typology. A type is a prophetic picture of Christ's person and work. It is a real person, place, object, event, etc., which God ordained to act as a predictive pattern or resemblance of Christ's person and work. A type is distinguished from an allegory by the following characteristics: (i) Its words may concern a story, an object, a person, or an event; (ii) The story, object, etc., is true, real and factual; (iii) The same truth is found in both the type and the antitype (fulfilment);

(iv) The same truth is enlarged, heightened and clarified in the antitype.

Example: The Passover lamb was a type of Christ. The Passover was a real event. The truths of substitutionary sacrifice and redemption by blood were found in both the type and the antitype. These truths were enlarged, heightened and clarified in the antitype. The antitype was the God-man — not just a lamb; and he redeemed from spiritual and eternal bondage — not just physical and temporary bondage.

While types and predictive prophecy are forward-looking in nature, they differ in form. A type prefigures using pictures, while a predictive prophecy uses words. Also, predictive prophecy is usually clearer than a type. A prediction simply tells the future, while a type has a meaning and significance even apart from anything in the future, and therefore is more complicated.

c. Presence

There are various occasions in the Old Testament when God appears and speaks to man. As God is invisible and only appears and speaks to sinners through his Son (Exod. 33:20; John 1:18), we must conclude that these appearances were the pre-incarnate Son of God, sometimes appearing as an angel and other times in human form (not flesh). We can learn much about Christ's person and work from these appearances.

d. Providence

When preaching about Old Testament characters and events, we must remember that they are all part of redemptive history; they are all part of the history that points to and leads to Christ. We must never separate these smaller narratives from the overarching narrative. Each person and incident is involved in the great outworking of God's plan to defeat the serpent and save his people.

Greidanus distinguishes the step from original message to 'fuller sense' as follows:

> Having gained insight into the immediate purpose of a book or passage, with biblical literature one must proceed a step further by inquiring after the ultimate purpose of a passage. We may call this ultimate purpose 'God's purpose', as long as we remember that the inspired human author's immediate purpose was also God's purpose. But God's ultimate purpose can be much broader and farther reaching than the relatively limited, immediate purpose of the human author. This broader, all-encompassing purpose becomes evident especially when a book or letter is interpreted in the context of the whole canon.[10]

e. People

Hebrews 1-10 sets forth Christ in all his glory. Hebrews 11 then sets forth the heroic faith of the Old Testament believers. Implicitly and explicitly we are being told that their faith was faith in Christ. So, when we are preaching about them we must remember that, like us, they were saved by grace alone through faith in Christ alone.

f. Precepts

God's law should never be preached as the way to salvation. Its purpose was to show the people's need of salvation and also the appropriate response to salvation — grateful obedience. That's why God's law is set in a redemptive context in both Exodus 19:4 and Exodus 20:2. The Lamb came before the Law. The pattern was redemption, relationship, response and reward. God's redemption brought them into relationship with him, and they were to express their gratitude by responding with grateful obedience, to which God would further add his blessing.

2. What are the applications in the area of faith or action?

Later I will devote a whole chapter to application. However, I agree with Douglas Stuart that practical application should also be part of the exegetical process. As we previously noted, the exegete's responsibility does not stop with the past — what the text meant. He must also go on and ask what it means now for Christians and non-Christians, young and old, the individual and the church, etc. Is this a passage of consolation or rebuke? Is this a truth to be believed or a duty to be done, etc.?

Example: Psalm 77 is a suitable model of prayer and practice for those who are depressed today.

3. Is there anything controversial in the text?

If there is something in the text that Christians have disagreed upon, study each view's strengths and weaknesses and defend the view best supported by Scripture.

Example: The prophecies of Ezekiel 40-48 regarding a rebuilt temple in Jerusalem have been taken literally by some Christians, and symbolically by others.

4. What do commentators say?

I've put this last because it is important to become an exegete of Scripture rather than a collator of others' thoughts. There may be times when a preacher is simply stumped very early in the exegetical process. In such cases it may be wise to consult a commentator or two just to get started. However, usually sermons are far fresher and more interesting if commentaries are read later in the process.

Disciplined and determined use of the questions in this chapter usually produce plenty of sermon material to work with. And that should also minimize the temptation of simply cutting and pasting from commentaries and sermons. Further, when the preacher forms his own thoughts and uses his own words, he will greatly reduce dependence on a manuscript when preaching. The more thoughts and ideas that are borrowed from others, the harder it is to remember them and express them when preaching.

While on the subject of 'cutting and pasting' it is often a fine line between learning from someone and simply copying their work without acknowledgement. No one expects preachers to verbally footnote everything they have gleaned from commentaries, etc. Also, sermon preparation is often a hurried and messy process in which we can often lose track of sources, etc. However, there is a significant moral difference between that and simply and very deliberately copying large chunks of other people's words or even sermon structures — without acknowledgement. 'You shall not steal' also applies in the preacher's study.

With these caveats in place, let me now say that every preacher should build up a library of reliable commentators on the text. It is good to read the mature conclusions of others in order to check our own conclusions. It may also stimulate fresh lines of enquiry. While depending on commentaries alone will generally produce stale and predictable sermons, depending on our own mind alone will eventually have the same effect. Some preachers boast that they never read commentaries or sermons. Their congregations often wish that they would!

Some points to look for in commentaries are given by Douglas Stuart:

> Have the conclusions of other scholars helped you to change your analysis in any way? Do other scholars analyze the passage or any aspects of it in a manner that is more incisive or that leads to a more satisfying set of conclusions? Do they organize their exegesis in a better way? Do they give consideration to implications you hadn't even considered? Do they supplement your own findings?[11]

CONCLUSION

At this point, some may say, 'At last, finished!' However, may I suggest that you now go through the whole process again! This is part of what I call the exegetical spiral. Martin Luther compared it to gathering apples:

> First I shake the whole tree, that the ripest may fall. Then I climb the tree and shake each limb, and then each branch and then each twig, and then I look under each leaf.

So back to the twigs and then the leaves!

4. VARIATION

VARYING THE SERMONS

If a preacher's sermons were gathered together into one pie, and then organized into category slices, how many slices would there be, and how big or small would each slice be?

In this chapter I will highlight and describe various sermon-category slices to help answer the question: 'Is the preacher preaching the whole "cake" of Scripture?' An awareness of the various kinds of sermon that may be preached challenges the preacher to vary his style and content, and so prevent monotonous sameness. Or it may help to highlight gaps that may be filled by concentrated study in that particular area.

Although the question of slice size will be touched upon, the variables of preacher, hearer, time, place and needs are too diverse to give any concrete rules. Answers to this question should be constantly and prayerfully sought from the great Shepherd of the sheep.

One point we might make before considering slice size is the need for a balanced selection of texts from Old Testament and New Testament; and in the New Testament from both the Gospels and the Epistles. If we might divide Scripture into three main divisions — the Old Testament, the Gospels, and the

Epistles — a general rule of thumb might be that texts should be drawn in roughly equal proportion from these three sources.

One last word of qualification before we present a classification of the different types of sermon: it should be noted that the distinctions are not always clear-cut and will often overlap. However, they are still useful if we remember that we are talking about general emphasis more than distinct and separate categories.

THE SLICES

The doctrinal sermon

A doctrinal sermon presents the facts and truths of the Bible's theology. It involves systematic and methodical instruction in the great doctrines of Christianity with a view to believing and doing. As the Reformers said, 'Doctrines must be preached practically, and duties doctrinally.' Charles Spurgeon wrote:

> Sermons should have real teaching in them, and their doctrine should be solid, substantial, and abundant... Nothing can compensate for the absence of teaching; all the rhetoric in the world is but as chaff to the wheat in contrast to the gospel of our salvation.[1]

One tendency to avoid is to try and preach a whole doctrine in one sermon. This results in abstract, vague and uninteresting sermons that only deal with generalities. John Broadus said,

> To choose some one aspect of a great subject is usually far better, as there is thus much better opportunity for the speaker to work out something fresh, and much better prospect of making the hearers take a lively interest in the

subject as a whole... Take it as a general rule, the more narrow the subject, the more thoughts you will have.[2]

Example 1: Instead of preaching on the atonement in general, the subject could be divided into various sermons entitled: (1) The need for atonement; (2) The nature of the atonement; (3) The extent of the atonement; (4) The beneficiaries of the atonement; (5) The effects of the atonement.

Example 2: Another approach might be to use a concordance to list the different verses relating to repentance, and be led by these texts into a careful and varied treatment of the various aspects revealed in them.

This thought from John Broadus should motivate and encourage us:

> The preacher who can endeavour to make doctrinal truth interesting as well as intelligible to his congregation, and gradually bring them to a good acquaintance with the doctrines of the Bible, is rendering them an inestimable service.[3]

Theistic sermons

This may seem a strange idea; shouldn't all sermons be theistic? There are two points to be underlined here. First, sermons should be focused on God — his nature, his demands, his provisions — rather than on human needs and desires. Second, theistic preaching must be balanced, preaching the whole God, as well as the whole counsel of God. If preaching reflects the scriptural balance, then neither the Father, the Son, nor the Holy Spirit will be neglected.

Example: In some circles the Holy Spirit may be overemphasized, but in others he may be under-represented. What proportion of sermons should be focused on each of the persons of the Godhead? Will the proportions vary depending on the congregation?

Apologetic sermons

Apologetic preaching involves the defence of scriptural doctrine and exposure of false views, with the ultimate aim of protecting the flock. It deals with questions such as: 'Is God there?'; 'How can I know God?'; 'Why does God allow suffering?'; 'What about the unevangelized heathen?'

There are certain dangers in such sermons. First, they must avoid the implication that the truthfulness of Christianity is open to question. Second, care must be taken not to suggest difficulties previously unknown and then failing to adequately address and remove them. Third, preachers should remember that the argument for Christianity is cumulative and cannot be presented in its entirety in one sermon.

Example: The use of evidences to support six-day creation and the exposure and refutation of evolution.

Controversial sermons

While apologetic sermons are concerned with the defence of Christianity from attacks coming from outside the church, 'controversial' or 'polemical' sermons are concerned with errors and heresies from within the church.

Preachers must be willing to contend for the faith (Jude 3) and hold fast to the form of sound words (2 Tim. 1:13). There are two extremes to be avoided here: the false charity that never fights for anything, and the love of conflict that fails to distinguish between fundamental and secondary issues. Broadus portrays the required balance:

> It would seem to be a just principle that a preacher should never go out of his way to find a controversial matter, nor go out of his way to avoid it. He who continually shrinks from conflict should stir himself up to faithfulness; he who is by nature belligerent, should cultivate forbearance and courtesy.[4]

Alexander warned against 'preaching with a contentious spirit, or so as to produce such a spirit.'

Example: Sermons on the subjects and modes of baptism.

Practical

Although we previously said that even doctrinal sermons should aim at the practical, there are some sermons that are especially practical, dealing with the Christian's duties toward God and others. Again we emphasize the need for balance here, a need highlighted by Dabney who said,

> The exclusive preaching of doctrine to professed Christians tends to cultivate an Antinomian spirit. The exclusive inculcation of duties fosters self-righteousness. The edification of the Church, then, demands the diligent intermixture of both kinds.[5]

Practical sermons should not only expose and condemn wrong living, but also encourage and direct God-honouring living.

They should be specific and not general, abstract or vague. Liberty of conscience should be recognized, and the motivation should be love-centred not law-centred.

Example: Sermons on many of the Proverbs, or the latter parts of Paul's Epistles.

Political sermons

Political sermons do not present a party-line, but teach the Christian view on the great questions affecting the State and public morals.

Example: Sermons on the evils of abortion, or on the biblical conditions for a just war.

Historical/biographical sermons

Historical sermons focus on the many personalities or events that fill the pages of Scripture. It is most significant that God has chosen to present most of the doctrines of the Bible in narrative form rather than in systematic, catechetical form. Broadus explains:

> Nothing so interests us all as a person. No inanimate object, or general proposition, will make much impression upon mankind at large, unless it is personified or impersonated, or invested with some personal interest... A celebrated lecturer on history once stated in conversation that he found it difficult to interest a popular audience, if he presented merely historical events, periods or lessons. These must be associated with some person.[6]

There are two cautions to bear in mind when preaching historical sermons. First, the importance of having a sufficient background knowledge of the history, geography and culture of the Bible if we are to present the scenes, events and people in a vivid and graphic way. Second, we need to remember that all biblical personalities and events point towards that one person, and one event of Christ's person and work.

Example: The covenant with Abraham in Genesis 12 or 15, pointing towards the ultimate seed and sacrifice of Christ.

Experiential sermons

Experiential (sometimes called 'experimental') sermons describe the varied spiritual experiences of Christian men and women as they receive the gospel and live for Christ in the midst of the trials and triumphs of life. Experiential preaching is rooted in Scripture, but need not confine itself to the Bible for illustrations of Christian experience. There are examples in church history, the preacher's own life, and the experiences of other Christians he knows.

Example 1: A sermon that describes conviction of sin, how it is wrought, the causes of it, the effects of it.

Example 2: A sermon that seeks to assure and comfort the hearts of God's fearful people.

Topical sermons

Topical sermons need not be tied to one verse or passage but may include consideration of a number of verses on a biblical topic. However, there is a real danger of topical preaching becoming simply a moral commentary on the events and topics of the day, making the source book the newspaper rather than the Bible. Irvin Busenitz explains how even topical preaching should be expository.

> Just as verse-by-verse preaching is not necessarily expository, preaching that is *not* verse-by-verse is not necessarily *non-expository*. Granted, *some* topical approaches are not expository, but such *need not* and certainly *should not* be the case. No book deals with topics that directly impact daily life more than the Bible. Thus, to be effective, all topical preaching and teaching, whether the topic be thematic, theological, historical, or biographical, must be consumed with expounding the Word.[7]

A topical sermon may take a topic from the world and bring the Bible's teaching to bear on it. Or it may select a biblical topic and organize the Bible's teaching on it.

Example 1: A tsunami, or a notable accident providing the basis of a sermon on the need for repentance and preparation for eternity. Or perhaps a sermon on the deity of Christ will bring together all the texts that help to defend and prove this.

Example 2: Several aspects of a truth can be brought together:

> Each man shall bear his own burden (Gal. 6:5);
> Bear one another's burdens (Gal. 6:2);
> Cast your burden on the LORD (Ps. 55:22).

Evangelistic sermons

While all sermons should contain an appeal to the unconverted in the congregation, evangelistic sermons are aimed largely or wholly at the unconverted. This will involve the application of the law's threatenings against their sin, the presentation of God's provision of a Saviour, the need for repentance and faith, and the urgency of the moment. Lloyd-Jones argued that there should be at least one sermon a week of an evangelistic nature, in addition to preaching to the believer in an experiential manner, and also in a more didactic instructional manner.[8]

W. E. Sangster says that the whole aim of an evangelistic sermon is to persuade the will. 'Evangelical preaching,' he said, 'is preaching for a verdict.' It still involves teaching and explanation, but it is more than that. It also includes argument and persuasion.

Example: A sermon on the Philippian jailer's question, 'What must I do to be saved?'

Discriminatory sermons

Discriminatory preaching identifies and distinguishes the characteristic marks of the saint and the sinner. In a sense it anticipates the final separation of the sheep from the goats based on the evidences of grace or the lack of it in the lives of the hearers. In a sermon Archibald Alexander said,

> It is much to be regretted that this accurate discrimination in preaching has gone so much out of use in our times. It is but seldom that we hear a discourse from the pulpit which is calculated to afford much aid to Christians in ascertaining their own true character; or which will serve

to detect the hypocrite and formalist, and drive them from all their false refuges.[9]

Example: A sermon on any one of the beatitudes that set forth the marks of a citizen of the kingdom of heaven.

Book sermons

It may be appropriate to take a whole book of Scripture as a text. A bird's-eye view can sometimes reveal more than a microscopic view. Sangster suggested that such a sermon might prove a fitting introduction to an expository series on a book.

> Let him steer the plane, therefore, that his hearers may see in outline, but in wholeness, the meaning of the Almighty in this piece of canonical writing; let him leave them hugging the warm thought to their hearts that they now understand Hosea or Jonah, James or Jude, and then let him venture on to the harder and longer books as their eagerness for more gives him encouragement. Such a preliminary sermon should always precede any detailed exposition of a book. To attempt to teach the physical geography of a country without putting a map before the pupils would be foolish. It is not less foolish in a preacher. The expositor of the Word must know both how to draw and how to display a large map.[10]

Genre sermons

The same truth can be taught through different genres of Scripture, through the poetry of the Psalms or the compelling logic of Paul's Epistles.

Example: A sermon on assurance could be based on Job's experience in Job 19:25-27 or on the more doctrinal Romans 8:15-16.

SUMMARY

This checklist should be used to regularly review the diet the preacher is serving up to his hearers. God's guidance should be sought to ensure that he is preaching the whole counsel of God in the proportions required for his situation and people. Varied sermon genres should help produce varied sermon content and preaching styles.

5. INTRODUCTION

BEGINNING THE SERMON

As 'God is not the author of confusion' but of order and structure, any sermon that claims to set forth God should be made in his image, i.e. with order and structure. Sermon structure and order will also help the preacher to preach and the hearers to hear, as they are both made in the image of God.

Just as a tree is made up of roots, a trunk with branches, and fruit, so most sermons are made up of an introduction, an exposition, and a conclusion. In this chapter we will dig into the roots by looking at how to introduce a sermon.

We will consider the necessity of an introduction, the negatives of an introduction, and the nature of an introduction.

THE NECESSITY OF AN INTRODUCTION

There are three reasons why our sermons should have an introduction.

Ordinary human experience

In our ordinary everyday social contact with other people we usually begin with a gradual introduction that deals with names, health, weather, etc., before we start the main topic of conversation. Indeed, we would consider it rude and offensive for someone to abruptly announce the topic of conversation and launch into it.

Sinful human experience

The preacher has to remember that he is speaking on subjects that the depraved human heart opposes. Even Christians often arrive in church with worldly thoughts and feelings, their souls chilled and deadened by everyday life in this world. Though the preacher may have mastered his subject and been warmed by it, few of his hearers are like this. Dabney said, 'When he is all fire and they as yet are ice, a sudden contact between his mind and theirs will produce rather a shock and revulsion than sympathetic harmony.'[1]

It is usually necessary then to introduce the subject of the sermon like a slowly rising sun rather than as a sudden searchlight. We have to spend a little time building bridges, initiating interest, demonstrating relevance, etc.

Archibald Alexander warned his students to take great care in preparing their introductions:

> It is a great mistake to suppose that the introduction and application of a sermon require little study. Perhaps they require the exercise of invention and ingenuity more than any other part of a sermon.[2]

The significance of an introduction, especially for new or unconverted hearers, is hugely disproportionate to its length. As Sangster counselled, the first impression may be the only impression:

> It is impossible to exaggerate the importance of the beginning of the sermon. Most of our hearers give us their attention at the start. However convinced they may be that preaching is boring, hope springs eternal and the thought lingers in the mind of the most blasé that perhaps on *this* occasion something of the awful majesty and arresting power they would associate with a message from God may be evident in what the preacher has to say. If he does not take firm grip of their attention in the first few minutes, how can he hope to hold it to the end?[3]

Hearers' expectations

Richard Mayhue argues that busy pastors will tend to focus their limited preparation time on their exegesis and structure. As a result introductions, illustrations and conclusions tend to be neglected. In contrast, the congregation eagerly looks forward to how its pastor will handle these elements of the message.

> The relationship of seasonings and sauces to gourmet cooking parallels the role of introductions, illustrations, and conclusions in preaching. The main meal, or the message, should never be eclipsed by secondary features; nonetheless, these garnishings can dramatically enhance the flavour/interest level of a meal/message well prepared in other respects.[4]

THE NEGATIVES OF AN INTRODUCTION

What should be avoided when a sermon is introduced?

Don't be too long

To avoid wearying people and unbalancing the sermon, an introduction should contain only one main thought. Dabney put it memorably: 'There is no need of a porch to enter a porch: we desire to step at once from the porch into the house.'[5]

Preachers should be especially careful about long introductions when preaching from narratives. They should not just repeat the story that many may already be familiar with, and all have just heard read a few minutes before. Sangster counsels:

> Cut into the subject with sharp, terse phrases. Resist, as you would resist the devil, that awful tendency to drag. Let the people feel in your whole manner that you have something most important to say and you simply cannot waste words.[6]

Don't be too showy

Attempts to display learning or be sensational will usually be counter-productive.

Don't be too ambitious

Trying to link a distant event or saying with the subject of the sermon by a long series of elaborate logical leaps will seem ridiculous to many hearers. The introduction and sermon must be clearly and easily linked.

Don't be too personal

A personal story may be acceptable and useful from time to time, but not as a regular feature.

Don't be too loud

Some preachers think that if they shout loud enough and long enough, people will pay attention. Unfortunately they soon exhaust themselves and their hearers.

Don't be too predictable

One writer has argued that a good introduction to a sermon would only be good for that sermon and for no other. That is probably going a bit too far, but if most of our introductions are adaptable to other sermons, then they probably are too general and vague. Stereotypical and predictable introductions should be avoided. Sometimes, but not often, it may be useful to give a brief introduction before reading the text.

Don't steal the sermon's thunder

The introduction should pave the way for the sermon, not repeat it.

Don't be apologetic

Preachers must not introduce their sermons with an apology for themselves or their sermons, however poor they may be. Preachers are authorized and authoritative ambassadors of

Christ and must convey that, rather than seek easy sympathy that eventually turns into contempt.

Don't flatter

Preachers who regularly begin by flattering their audiences will soon be the target of their criticism.

Don't be offensive

Due regard should be given to the age and sensitivities of the congregation so that offence is not unnecessarily given and ears closed before hardly leaving the blocks.

THE NATURE OF AN INTRODUCTION

Before we look at the various types of sermon introduction, we will briefly consider what stage in the sermon preparation process introductions should be prepared. The fact that this chapter appears after chapters on selecting and expositing the text should give a clue. While on some rare occasions the introduction might be prepared first, it is most common to prepare it after exegesis is completed.

The 'Pay attention' introduction

The preacher begins with a solemn call for attention to an important subject. This was done in Scripture by Moses (Deut. 4:1), Stephen (Acts 7:2), and the Lord (Matt. 15:10). However, it will lose its force if often repeated. It is usually best to say something that will interest rather than demand interest. 'What is the best way', asked a young preacher of an older one, 'to get the attention of the congregation?' 'Give 'em something to attend to,' was the gruff reply.

The contextual introduction

The preacher explains the historical background, and the connections and relations between the text and the surrounding material. This helps to keep the text central and upfront.

Example: A sermon on Romans 12:1 will connect the 'therefore' with what the 'therefore' is based upon — chapters 1-11.

The background introduction

The preacher describes the history, geography, or culture of the people and places relevant to the text or the context. Two principles to keep in mind here are 'summarize' and 'modernize'. By summarize, I mean that he should not get lost in the detail, and so lose precious preaching time — and the congregation's attention. Rather, he should focus on the verse's relation to the main historical dates. By modernize, I mean bring the past into the present by showing what the events would look like if they happened here and now.

Example: Imagine Edinburgh besieged by a vast army. The local politicians have been captured and the judges have been publicly flogged. The population is starving and is being rounded up for a long sail and a forced march to a foreign and unfriendly land. In the midst of this a minister of the gospel begins preaching in the open air. He is the same minister who had been warning the people of Edinburgh that their sins would bring God's judgement upon them. And now he opens his mouth again. The people expect to hear, 'I told you so!' Instead, he preaches a sermon of hope and optimism. He announces that God will yet raise up a great leader to rescue and restore them. Moreover he affirms that this mighty deliverer will come from a tiny and virtually unknown village in the Western Isles. Now travel back in time to about 700 BC. Substitute Jerusalem for Edinburgh, Assyria for the foreign armies, Micah for the minister of the gospel, and Bethlehem for the insignificant village. This is the situation we find in Micah chapter 5. And the verse we would especially like to consider is verse 2.

The principle introduction

The preacher will begin with a biblical principle that is familiar to the hearers and proceed to show in the sermon how this particular example proves the principle.

Example: Principle: Love makes everything easier. Text: 'So Jacob served seven years for Rachel, and they seemed only a few days to him because of the love he had for her' (Gen. 29:20).

The example introduction

This is the reverse of the 'principle introduction'. The preacher begins with a real-life example that illustrates a principle he is about to preach upon. Care must be taken to ensure that the example is not out of place in a sermon.

Example: Dabney recounts how a New Year's sermon on the text, 'This year you shall die' (Jer. 28:16), was introduced by the statement that both Jonathan Edwards and Samuel Davies preached from this passage at the beginning of the years in which they were unexpectedly cut off by death.

A contrast introduction

In this type of introduction a commonly held worldly principle or well-known example of worldly conduct is contrasted with scriptural principles or examples which are then preached upon.

Example: 'You have put gladness in my heart, more than in the season that their grain and wine increased' (Ps. 4:7). The world offers you a good time *but* the Lord offers you a glad heart.

A topical introduction

The preacher can often gain attention and arouse interest by preaching on a subject of current national or ecclesiastical interest.

Example: 'It is the LORD. Let Him do what seems good to Him' (1 Sam. 3:18). As we read the newspapers and watch our televisions, we see that the world is full of tragedies. Our own lives are often affected by tragedies. How should we respond?

An advantages introduction

A sermon may be introduced by highlighting the spiritual or practical advantages of studying a specific subject. This is especially useful when the subject may be particularly sensitive or offensive to the natural heart of men and women.

Example: 'The people who know their God shall be strong, and carry out great exploits' (Dan. 11:32b). The preacher could say, 'We are beginning a series on the attributes of God. Let me give you six reasons why we should study the Bible's teaching on this...'

A seasonal introduction

Reference to a particular time of year in the national, local, or ecclesiastical calendar may profitably introduce a sermon.

Example: 'Honour your father and your mother' (Exod. 20:12). 'Yesterday the Queen published her New Years Honours list. Soldiers, athletes, footballers, singers, etc., were honoured. What about your mother and father? Have you honoured them?'

An apologetic introduction

This is not a contradiction of the earlier negative: 'Don't be apologetic.' This is a reference to the need for the preacher to confront error and heresy both in the church and outside it. He may begin with a reference to a person, a cult, or an organization that holds a particular view and then go on to prove its falsehood and assert the biblical truth.

Example: 'If anyone wills to do His will, he shall know concerning the doctrine, whether it is from God or whether I speak on My own authority' (John 7:17). Many people say they are agnostics. Regarding God's existence, they say, 'I don't know and no one can know.' But Jesus says that if we do his truth, we will know (John 3:21).

A question introduction

Here, the preacher poses a question about the text, the people, the church, or the world.

Example: W. E. Sangster tells of how 'Few who heard J. N. Figgis preach his last sermon before the University of Cambridge ever forgot the way he began. It was 2 June 1918. After nearly four years of gruelling war, the Allies were being driven back again. Miles that had taken months to win were lost in hours. In that tense atmosphere of national fear he started with the text: "The LORD sitteth upon the flood; yea, the LORD sitteth King for ever" (Ps. 29:10, AV), and he began at once with one tense question: "*Does he? Does he?*" That was enough. He was in.'[7]

A quotation introduction

A sermon may be introduced with a striking quotation by a Christian, or even a non-Christian.

Example: 'What kind of child will this be?' (Luke 1:66). Dr E. T. Sullivan said, 'The greatest forces in the world are not the earthquakes and the thunderbolts: the greatest forces in the world are babies.'

A letter introduction

A preacher might read part of a letter he received, or even published newspaper correspondence. In the case of the former he must either make sure that his correspondent cannot be identified by what is read, or, preferably, his permission to read the letter has been granted.

Example: Before I preached on the difficult problem of the Israelites killing so many Canaanites in obedience to God's command, I read a letter I received about it:

> I'm still left with the difficult problem of Jericho... My question would be, why were the Israelites so aggressive? I'm sure in those days there was plenty of land for all, was it really necessary to butcher the whole city bar one family? Yes, I know that the penalty for sin was death, but couldn't they have tried to at least convert them? This [murderous attitude] is the attitude the Muslims had when Mohammed was trying desperately to start his religion. This kind of story is one which many people use to preach against Christianity, especially Muslims. How can we call Muslims bloodthirsty? How can we call ourselves peaceful!? If we take the [Old Testament] Israeli example of their destruction of Jericho, do we cut the throats of those that don't believe?

The question, then, is, 'Should we kill our spiritual enemies?' Or, in the context of our letter-writer, 'Should we kill Muslims?'

A statistical introduction

Statistics about the state of religion or morals in the country could be used to highlight a problem that the text addresses.

Example: 'For the great day of His wrath has come, and who is able to stand?' (Rev. 6:17). 'Our society is becoming angrier. Consumer Research Poll found that 90% feel they are far angrier than they were ten years ago, and 10% get angry every day. But our text tells us that however angry our society is today, there is an even greater day of anger ahead...'

A 'What would you do?' introduction

This introduction would describe a difficult situation or dilemma and ask: 'What you would do?', before going on to show what the Bible says we should do.

Example: 'What would you do if a woman were brought to you having committed open adultery. Jesus said, "Neither do I condemn you; go and sin no more" (John 8:11).'

CONCLUSION

Just as a tree has roots to place and secure the tree in the ground, so a sermon must have an introduction to place and secure it in the minds of the congregation. In the next chapter we will consider the sermon's 'trunk' and 'branches' — its organization.

6. ORGANIZATION (I)

THE PRINCIPLES OF SERMON ORGANIZATION

In the last chapter we studied sermon introductions, which we likened to the roots of a tree. We would now like to look at the trunk, the main body of the sermon. I am assuming that the work of textual exegesis has already been done (see chapter 3). What we are concerned with now is organizing the resulting material.

In this chapter we will examine the principles of sermon organization, and in the next we will look at the practice of sermon organization. In other words, we will look at the theory and then at a number of practical examples.

Structured

The preacher is described as, 'a worker who does not need to be ashamed, rightly dividing the word of truth' (2 Tim. 2:15). This means that a major part of the preacher's task is to divide his interpretation of the word of God into appropriate blocks of material and present them in logical sequence.

W. E. Sangster conceded 'that a sermon can be without form and — such is the grace of God — not be utterly void.' Nevertheless, he added, this 'borders on the miraculous. No sermon is really strong which is not strong in structure.' Just as bones without flesh make a skeleton, so flesh without bones makes a jellyfish. And neither bony skeletons nor jellyfish make good sermons.[1]

Sometimes the structure will be obvious before the preacher even begins to 'question' his text, sometimes it will arise as he works on it, and sometimes it will only arise after the work of exegesis is completed. In sermon preparation, the preacher should be constantly seeking a structure. And even when one emerges, the question should be, 'Is this the best one?' The preacher must be prepared to dispense with his initial structure if another emerges which better presents the subject.

The major benefit of structure, apart from helping the preacher to present his material, is that it greatly helps listeners to remember what they heard. Some will say that if he feels his message enough then why not just preach it from the heart without any conscious effort to order out thoughts and feelings. Glen Knecht's argument against this is based on the doctrine of God:

God is a God of order. He did not create everything all at once, but in sequence. He grouped things in classes and created like things on the same days. He revealed Himself in stages and brought all things to readiness before He gave the crowning piece of His revelation, the Lord Jesus Christ. Full of ardor, God is also full of order in what He does. We must copy God in this order, realizing that the source of His order is His love. It is because He loves us that He adapts His work and His words to our condition and speaks to us in such a way that we can understand and apply what we learn of Him. Our ardor to proclaim

His Word and to see the fruit of His Spirit's work in the world is also an ardor of love. It is because we love Him and others that we preach. Our love makes us translate our ardor into order when it comes to the proclaiming of the Word of God. Giving order to substance is an act of loving the hearer and loving the author of the revelation. It is the second mile that is the mile of love. 'Good thoughts abound,' Pascal reminds us, 'but the art of organizing them does not.' The difference between the first and second mile preacher is that one has powerful thoughts issuing from a burning heart, and the other, having the same truths and as full an ardour, adds to his love the strenuous effort of moulding them into a shape that will be helpful and retainable to those who listen.[2]

Simple

Sermon structures ought to be as simple as possible, with as few divisions as possible. Multiple divisions tend to attract attention more to the structure of the message rather than to the message itself. They also tend to over-tax the memory and make the listening exercise more mind-centred than heart-centred, more cerebral than spiritual, more like a lecture than a sermon.

What is the ideal number of divisions? Although there is no hard and fast rule, three divisions is the most common, probably because it presents the material with a beginning, a middle and an end. Dr Martyn Lloyd-Jones cautions:

> Never force a division. And do not add to the number of divisions for the sake of some kind of completeness that you have in your mind or in order to make it conform to your usual practice. The headings should be natural and appear to be inevitable.[3]

In *Princeton and Preaching* James Garretson, reflecting on Archibald Alexander's methodology, wrote:

> ...minute division of a text, or unnecessary elaboration of points that are obvious, serve no purpose if preaching is to be useful and edifying. Hearers will be either annoyed at the unnecessary minutiae, or despondent that they cannot remember the divisions and sub-points. It is an interesting observation that some of the greatest sermons are deceptively simple in design and development. Simplicity in design, organization and development is the mark of a great communicator. Complexity confounds — simplicity satisfies.[4]

Striking

The preacher should work at producing fresh and striking headings in order to arouse interest and aid memory. John Broadus said,

> So many sermons follow the beaten track, in which we can see all that is coming, as to make it a weary task even for devout hearers to listen attentively. One feels inclined to utter a plaintive cry, 'Worthy brother, excellent brother, if you could only manage to drive us sometimes over a different road, even if much less smooth, even if you do not know it very well — I am so tired of this!'[5]

It is worth taking as much time and effort as necessary here because the better the headings, the better people will remember and assimilate the truth. So seriously did Martyn Lloyd-Jones take this that he advised preachers to leave a sermon to be preached at another time if they did not settle on a satisfactory structure, especially if it was a particularly important sermon.

While arguing for striking and memorable structure, we must still remember that the purpose of any skeleton is to support the body, and keep itself largely out of view. The purpose of memorable headings is not so that your hearers remember the preacher but that they remember the message of God's Word.

Stated?

There has been much debate over how much should be stated at the beginning of a sermon. Some of the older writers argue for a concise statement of the sermon's theme and points before beginning the sermon. There are advantages and disadvantages to pre-announcement. While I usually favour stating the theme, I usually prefer not to pre-announce the sermon points. It removes the element of surprise and sometimes it may also make hearers switch off if they wrongly conclude from the headings that the sermon is not for them. Martyn Lloyd-Jones also worried that stating the points up front tended to focus people's attention on the form rather than the content of the message.

Pre-announcement might be a good idea if the structure will help the hearers follow a complex argument, or if it might stimulate interest rather than diminish it.

Whether the theme and points are stated at the beginning of a sermon or not, the theme and points should be crystal clear in the preacher's mind. It is especially important to work on a clear, comprehensive, concise sentence that presents the sermon theme. Dabney argued not only for a clear sermon theme, but also for a clear sermon aim:

> The speaker must have one main subject of discourse, to which he adheres with supreme reference throughout. But this is not enough. He must, second, propose to

himself one definite impression on the hearer's soul, to the making of which everything in the sermon is bent... Unity of discourse requires, then, not only singleness of a dominant subject, but also singleness of practical impression. To secure the former, see to it that the whole discussion may admit of reduction to a single proposition. To secure the latter, let the preacher hold before him, through the whole preparation of the sermon, the one practical effect intended to be produced upon the hearer's will.[6]

Charles Simeon believed that a clear sermon theme was 'the great secret of all composition for the pulpit'. In an anonymous article in the *Christian Observer* in December 1821, Simeon wrote:

Reduce your text to a simple proposition, and lay that down as the warp; and then make use of the text itself as the woof; illustrating the main idea by the various terms in which it is contained. Screw the word into the minds of your hearers. A screw is the strongest of all mechanical powers ... when it has turned a few times, scarcely any power can pull it out.[7]

J. H. Jowett went further:

I have a conviction that no sermon is ready for preaching ... until we can express its theme in a short, pregnant sentence as clear as a crystal. I find the getting of that sentence is the hardest, the most exacting and the most fruitful labour in my study ... I do not think any sermon ought to be preached, or even written, until that sentence has emerged, clear and lucid as a cloudless moon.[8]

All sermon divisions should serve the purpose of advancing the sermon theme.

Smooth

People must feel that they are moving towards the flowers and fruit at the top of the sermon tree. The sermon should move from point to point without gap or jar. The parts should fit well together and each should grow logically into the next. Negatives should precede positives, the abstract should precede the concrete, generals should precede specifics, and teaching should precede application.

Symmetrical

This does not mean that each division must be the same size. However, gross imbalance might indicate that the material is not rightly divided. That said, symmetry really means that each division should reflect the symmetry of the text. This may require the ruthless discarding of material, even otherwise helpful material. There is no need to be over-symmetrical in sub-points. Just because the first point had three sub-points that does not mean that all the other points must be similar.

Spoken

The division descriptions must be suited to spoken announcement. Logical divisions may help in preparation, but the preacher is a speaker and may have to adapt his divisions so that they suit listeners more than readers. This is why alliterative headings, or headings of the same length or rhythm are often helpful. Resist the urge for too much double alliteration (two words beginning with the same letters) and for sub-point alliteration.

Separate

The divisions should be distinct and not overlap with other divisions. Do not make a division without a difference, just to secure three points.

Spiritual

Sermon material should be organized throughout with a spiritual intent — with the aim of doing spiritual good. Archibald Alexander said,

> In order to do good by preaching, the attention of the audience must be gained and kept up; and some impression made on their feelings.[9]

This means that the instruction and teaching should be applied to the hearers in a relevant way throughout. Application wins interest for the information and vice versa. As Broadus said,

> The successive waves of emotion may thus rise higher and higher to the end. And besides, while thought produces emotion, it is also true that emotion reacts upon and quickens thought, so that impressive application of one division may secure for the next a closer attention.[10]

Scriptural

Although this is really the most important point of all, we put it last here for emphasis. In general, the sermon structure will arise obviously from the text of Scripture. Archibald Alexander puts this well:

> Ideally, sermon outlines will arise out of a text, after careful study of the context and meaning of the passage to be preached upon. Care must be taken not to impose an outline on a text that does not arise naturally from the text.[11]

Dr Martyn Lloyd-Jones said that the number of heads was much less important than that the 'heads must be there in your text, and they must arise naturally out of it.'[12]

CONCLUSION

One last 's' is 'struggle'. Organizing a sermon requires deep concentration, strenuous effort, prolonged quiet, and deep dependence on God. We can also learn to structure sermons by examining the sermons of the best preachers, by having our own structures critiqued by other preachers, and by studying logic.

Having considered some of the 'principles' of sermon organization in this chapter, in the next we will look at the 'practice'.

7. ORGANIZATION (2)

=== *THE PRACTICE*

OF SERMON ORGANIZATION ===

We will now take some of the principles of organization introduced in the previous chapter and put them into practice. We will look at various practical ways of organizing our sermons.

Nouns

Perhaps the easiest and most obvious structure is based upon the subjects in the verse or passage being studied.

Example: 'Rejoice with me, for I have found my sheep which was lost!' (Luke 15:6).

i.   The sheep's lostness
ii. The shepherd's love

Example: 'Then He turned to the woman and said to Simon, "Do you see this woman? I entered your house; you gave Me no water for My feet, but she has washed My feet with her tears and wiped *them* with the hair of her head'" (Luke 7:44ff).

i.   The sinner
ii. Simon
iii. The Saviour

Adjectives

The preacher may also use various adjectives to describe a person, an event, or an occasion in the text.

Example: 'Who is on the LORD's side?' (Exod. 32:26, KJV).

i.   A clear question
ii. An important question
iii. An urgent question
iv. A divisive question

Verbs

Another approach is to organize the sermon around the verbs found in the text.

Example: 'Will You not revive us again, that Your people may rejoice in You?' (Ps. 85:6).

i. A reviving
ii. A rejoicing

Example: 'He who covers his sins will not prosper, but whoever confesses and forsakes *them* will have mercy' (Prov. 28:13).

i. Covering sin
ii. Confessing sin

Outline points should be parallel in structure, i.e., built around the same part of speech (all nouns, all verbs, etc.).

Questions

A sermon can be structured around the questions that may be asked of the text.

Example: 'Seek the LORD while He may be found, call upon Him while He is near' (Isa. 55:6).

i. What is missing?
ii. Why should I search for this?
iii. Where should I search?
iv. When should I search?
v. How should I search?
vi. Who is to search?

Imperatives

If a text contains commands, then the sermon can easily be arranged around these commands.

Example: 'Go therefore and make disciples of all the nations, baptizing them in the name of the Father and of the Son and of the Holy Spirit, teaching them to observe all things that I have commanded you; and lo, I am with you always, *even* to the end of the age. Amen' (Matt. 28:19-20).

i.   Go
ii. Teach
iii. Baptize

Metaphor

The Bible is rich in metaphors and the suggestive imagery can help the preacher to form a structure.

Example: 'The LORD God is a sun' (Ps. 84:11).

Like the sun, God....

i.   Is hot
ii. Is huge
iii. Is high
iv. Is here
v.   Heals
vi. Gives happiness
vii. Hardens

Application

Instead of structuring our sermons around our exegesis, we can sometimes structure it around our application and support the application with our exegesis.

Example: 'Now when the devil had ended every temptation, he departed from Him until an opportune time. Then Jesus returned in the power of the Spirit to Galilee, and news of Him went out through all the surrounding region' (Luke 4:13-14).

i.   Temptation comes to the most holy
ii. Temptation is a test of faith
iii. Temptation is beaten by truth
iv. Temptation resisted is rewarded

Emotions

The different emotions expressed by Bible characters may provide sermons headings.

Example: 'Why are you cast down, O my soul? And why are you disquieted within me? Hope in God; for I shall yet praise Him, the help of my countenance and my God' (Ps. 42:11).

i. A sad soul
ii. A smiling soul

Contrasts

Contrasts can often provide a ready-made 'skeleton' for a sermon.

Example: 'For thus says the High and Lofty One who inhabits eternity, whose name *is* Holy: "I dwell in the high and holy *place,* with him *who* has a contrite and humble spirit, to revive the spirit of the humble, and to revive the heart of the contrite ones"' (Isa. 57:15).

i. God is far away in the high and holy heavens
ii. God is near in the humble human heart

Biography

Sermons on Bible characters may be organized around their various experiences.

Example: 'But you his son, Belshazzar, have not humbled your heart... Then the fingers of the hand were sent from Him, and this writing was written. And this is the inscription that was written: MENE, MENE, TEKEL, UPHARSIN. This *is* the interpretation of *each* word. MENE: God has numbered your kingdom, and finished it; TEKEL: You have been weighed in the balances, and found wanting; PERES: Your kingdom has been divided, and given to the Medes and Persians' (Dan. 5:22-28).

i.   His sins/folly
ii. His scare/fright
iii. His sentence/future

Responses

The different responses of different people to a situation can also structure a sermon.

Example: 'The kingdom of heaven is like a certain king who arranged a marriage for his son, and sent out his servants to call those who were invited to the wedding; and they were not willing to come...' (Matt. 22:2-3).

The responses:

i. Apathy
ii. Activity

iii. Aggression
iv. Acceptance

Example: 'Entreat me not to leave you...' (Ruth 1:13-17).

i.   A grieving widow
ii. A leaving widow
iii. A cleaving widow

Cause and effect

The effects of certain actions and attitudes can be traced to the original causes.

Example: 'And because lawlessness will abound, the love of many will grow cold' (Matt. 24:12).

i.   Iniquity abounding
ii. Love abating

Moral principles

The preacher may wish to draw out the moral principles latent in a passage and use these as his sermon headings.

Example: 'But Jesus said to him, "Put your sword in its place, for all who take the sword will perish by the sword"' (Matt. 26:52).

i.   The weapons of our warfare are not carnal but spiritual (2 Cor. 10:4);
ii. Blessed are the peacemakers (Matt. 5:9);

iii. Whoever sheds man's blood by man shall his blood be shed (Gen. 9:6);

iv. '"Vengeance is Mine, I will repay," says the Lord' (Rom. 12:19);

v. The Son of Man came to seek and to save that which was lost (Luke 19:10);

vi. The word of God is living and powerful and sharper than any two-edged sword (Heb. 4:12).

Textual

Sometimes the text will yield an obvious structure.

Example: 'Likewise you also, reckon yourselves to be dead indeed to sin, but alive to God in Christ Jesus our Lord' (Rom. 6:11).

i.   Reckon yourselves dead to sin
ii. Reckon yourselves alive to God

Example: 'We give thanks to God always for you all, making mention of you in our prayers, remembering without ceasing your work of faith, labour of love, and patience of hope in our Lord Jesus Christ in the sight of our God and Father, knowing, beloved brethren, your election by God' (1 Thess. 1:2-4).

i.   The 'how' of thanksgiving (v. 2b)
ii. The 'when' of thanksgiving (v. 3)
iii. The 'why' of thanksgiving (v. 4)

Past/present/future

A number of texts have temporal reference points that can also provide our sermon points.

Example: 'Truly, these times of ignorance God overlooked, but now commands all men everywhere to repent, because He has appointed a day on which He will judge the world in righteousness by the Man whom He has ordained. He has given assurance of this to all by raising Him from the dead' (Acts 17:30-31).

i.   The past: compassion
ii. The present: command
iii. The future: conclusion

Before and after

Related to the previous suggestion is the structure founded upon 'before' and 'after' comparisons.

Example: 'Truly, this only I have found: that God made man upright, but they have sought out many schemes' (Eccl. 7:29).

i.   God's good invention
ii. Man's bad invention

Causes, consequences, cures

The medical approach of cause, consequence and cure can be used to open up a text and structure a sermon.

Example: 'The poor will never cease from the land' (Deut. 15:11).

i.   The causes of poverty
ii. The consequences of poverty
iii. The cure of poverty

Question and answer

A verse or passage may ask and answer a question in such a way that a sermon can be built around.

Example: 'Who shall separate us from the love of Christ? ... Yet in all these things we are more than conquerors through Him who loved us...' (Rom. 8:35-37).

i.   Question: Who shall separate us from the love of Christ?
ii. Answer: Nothing

Pairs

A preacher should be on the lookout for 'pairs'.

Example: 'Enter by the narrow gate...' (Matt. 7:13-14).

i.   Two gates
ii. Two roads
iii. Two destinations

Positive and negative

Truth is often presented negatively and positively.

Example: 'Command those who are rich in this present age not to be haughty, nor to trust in uncertain riches but in the living God, who gives us richly all things to enjoy' (1 Tim. 6:17).

i.   Do not trust in uncertain riches
ii. Do trust in the certain God

Apologetic

Dr Martyn Lloyd-Jones was a classic exponent of the apologetic style of preaching (by which we mean defending the faith, rather than saying sorry for it). He was a brilliant exegete of Scripture, especially adept at identifying and communicating the essential truth of a text; but where he really excelled was in how he then presented that truth. He often began by developing an argument against the truth that he was presenting. Then he would systematically demolish the argument and establish in its place the biblical truth.

CONCLUSION

These are just some samples of the many and varied structures by which sermons may be organized. Preachers may want to review past sermons to identify other alternative organizing methods. Again, I return to the need for variation in presenting the truth.

8. APPLICATION (1)

THE PRINCIPLES OF APPLICATION

We will consider the principles of application in this chapter, and the practice of application in the next. But, before looking at the principles of application we will look at some definitions of what application is, and then briefly consider the scriptural warrant for application.

THE DEFINITION OF APPLICATION

Jay Adams wrote:

> Application is the ... process by which preachers make scriptural truths so pertinent to members of their congregations that they not only understand how these truths should effect changes in their lives but also feel obligated and perhaps even eager to implement those changes.[1]

Al Martin said,

> Application is the arduous task of suffusing the sermon with pointed, specific, and discriminating force to the conscience.

My own definition is:

Application is the process by which the unchanging principles of God's Word are brought into life-changing contact with people who live in an ever-changing world.

This may seem obvious. However, some exegetes of Scripture think that once they have explained the meaning of the text, their work is done. They make no attempt to determine what the text means now. Exegesis then becomes a merely academic and scholarly exercise detached from real life.

Other exegetes do have a desire to connect Scripture with real life, but believe that is the job of the Holy Spirit, not the preacher. They say, 'We explain the text and the Spirit applies it.' Douglas Stuart highlights the unfairness of this approach:

The exegete, who has come to know the passage best, refuses to help the reader or hearer of the passage at the very point where the reader's or hearer's interest is keenest. The exegete leaves the key function — response — completely to the subjective sensibilities of the reader or hearer, who knows the passage least.[2]

What is even more likely is that the hearers will do nothing at all. John Calvin noted:

If we leave it to men's choice to follow what is taught them, they will never move one foot. Therefore, the doctrine of itself can profit nothing at all.[3]

THE WARRANT FOR APPLICATION

As some preachers argue against personal application of Scripture, we need to show that application is warranted and justified by

Scripture. We do this by simply highlighting just some of the many examples of application that we find in the Bible itself.

Example 1: In Matthew 19:16-22 Christ applied the law to the rich young ruler.

Example 2: In Acts 2:22-39 Peter applied the prophetic Scriptures of the Old Testament to his generation (vv. 25-28; 34-35). His sermon intended to change his hearers. Notice how often he uses the second person (vv. 22, 23, 29, 33, 36). They respond: 'What shall we do?' (v. 37). Peter calls them to repentance and faith (vv. 38, 39).

Example 3: In 1 Corinthians 10:11 Paul says that the history of Israel was written as an example and admonition to all later generations.

Example 4: Paul affirms: 'For whatever things were written before were written for our learning, that we through the patience and comfort of the Scriptures might have hope' (Rom. 15:4).

So convinced was that great preacher Spurgeon of the necessity of application that he said, 'Where the application begins, there the sermon begins.'

Having made these preliminary points let us now look at the principles of application.

THE PRINCIPLES OF APPLICATION

Preaching passage

The faithful preacher bases his application not on anecdotes or inspiring stories, but on God's Word, and on that particular preaching passage. Douglas Stuart said,

An application should be just as rigorous, just as thorough, and just as analytically sound as any other step in the exegesis process. It cannot be merely tacked on to the rest of the exegesis as a sort of spiritual afterthought. Moreover it must carefully reflect the data of the passage if it is to be convincing. Your reader needs to see how you derived the application as the natural and final stage of the entire process of careful, analytical study of your passage.[4]

While focused on that particular preaching passage, preachers must also ensure that their application is consistent with the rest of Scripture. That will prevent building a false teaching or practice on an isolated or obscure text.

Primary

Preachers must not draw applications from the accidental, incidental, or coincidental parts of a passage, but from its essentials alone. This is especially important to bear in mind when preaching from historical narratives or parables. As the parables are usually making only one point, we must not found a doctrine or practice on one of the incidental points. An old Baptist minister used to tell young preachers, 'With parables, don't turn a monopod into a centipede!' One of the best ways of finding the primary application(s) of a particular passage is by asking, 'What was the original application, to the original audience, at the original time of writing?' Jay Adams wrote:

The truth God revealed in Scripture came in an applied form and should be reapplied to the same sort of people for the same purposes for which it was originally given. That is to say, truth should be applied today just as God originally applied it.[5]

Persistent

Although at times it may be appropriate to leave application to the conclusion of a sermon, it is usually best to apply throughout. Charles Bridges highlights the persistent application of history and doctrine throughout the book of Hebrews and concludes:

> The method of perpetual application, therefore, where the subject will admit of it, is probably best calculated for effect — applying each head distinctly...[6]

In *Truth Applied* Jay Adams speaks of applicatory introductions, as well as conclusions: 'It [application] should begin with the first sentence and continue throughout.'[7] This is going a bit far, but certainly there should be persistent application throughout, at least at the end of each sermon division.

Prepared

While many preachers will spend hours on preparing their exegesis, they will often spend little time on application. It is sometimes thought that while we must prepare the teaching part, we should simply rely on the Spirit for the application. But, remember the previously quoted words of Douglas Stuart:

> An application should be just as rigorous, just as thorough, and just as analytically sound as any other step in the exegesis process.

Unprepared application usually means repetitive application. Mentally tired after explaining the text, a preacher often defaults to the well-worn ruts of application he has travelled down time and again in the past.

One of the best ways to prepare applications is to pray over the sermon and to ask God how to apply it. God's Spirit knows the hearts of the hearers better than anyone, and he can reveal people's needs by his Spirit. A prayerful spirit while preaching can also result in God guiding a preacher to speak to specific needs in his hearers. Also, as the fear of man can disable application, we need to pray for constant deliverance from it.

Present

Applications should be up-to-date and relevant. There is no point in simply taking the applications made by the Puritans and Reformers and repeating them to our own modern congregations. Their applications were up-to-date when they made them, but many of them are now past their 'use by' date.

One of the greatest helps to application is keeping up-to-date with both the world we live in and the people we pastor. Only then can we know our hearers' concerns, interests, dangers, etc. Another way to improve application is to go through the congregation and try to describe each person with one word that characterizes their spiritual condition or status. That should produce a ready-made checklist of the various kinds of hearers in the congregation to focus application on.

To get started here are some *broad categories* of listeners to aim application at:

Christian/non-Christian, old/young, rich/poor, parents/children/singles, employer/employee, government/citizen, male/female, atheist/agnostic/persecutor.

And here are some *narrower categories* of people that may be found in some, many, or even all of each of the broader categories:

The sick, dying, afflicted, tempted, backslidden, hypocrite, anxious, immoral, lonely, discouraged, worried, tired, seeker, doubter, proud, bereaved, broken-hearted, convicted, etc.

Personal

Daniel Webster exclaimed: 'When a man preaches to me, I want him to make it a personal matter, a personal matter, a personal matter!'

What does this mean? Well, 'personal' application starts with the preacher applying the word to himself. Al Martin said,

Here is the main reason why there is so little applicatory preaching. Men are not applying the Word to their own hearts. A minister's life is the life of the minister.

However, what we want to focus on here especially is the importance of 'second-person' application. Let me summarize Jay Adams' excellent teaching on this in *Truth Applied*.[8]

Application may sometimes be in the 'first person'. There are times when the preacher will identify personally with the application. He will then speak in 'first-person' terms: '*We* must...'; '...died for *us*'; '*our* privilege is...' (e.g. Heb. 4:1, 11, 14, 16).

Application may also, at times, be in the 'third person'. For example, a sermon may be preached to young people on the duties of husbands or wives, when none of the hearers are yet married. The sermon will then speak in third-person terms: '*Husbands* will...'; 'When *wives* are...'; '*She* usually knows...' Perhaps there will be application concerning the errors of false religions and the cults, again in third-person terms: '*They* wrongly believe and teach...' (e.g. Titus 1:10-16).

However, while first-person and third-person applications are both scriptural and, at times, appropriate, the majority of applications should be in the 'second person': '*You* must...', '*You* should understand...', '*Your* experience...' (e.g. John 3:7; Rom. 12:1). This is not to exclude the preacher from the application. However, it does reflect the fact that the preacher holds an 'office'. He is not preaching in his own right, but as an ambassador sent by God to deliver a message to the people of God. He, therefore, speaks 'in Christ's stead', as Christ himself would speak to the people were he present. Such practice will avoid the common scenario highlighted by Al Martin:

> Many sermons are like unaddressed, unsigned letters which if 100 people read it they would not think the contents concerned them.

The preacher's hearers must know that they are being addressed personally and even individually. As Charles Bridges said, 'Preaching, in order to be effective, must be reduced from vague generalities, to a tangible, individual character — coming home to every man's business, and even his bosom.'[9] This is another way we can discern whether we are preaching or simply lecturing.

The newspaper editor of the *Brooklyn Eagle* kept a desktop notice saying, 'Always remember that a dog fight in Brooklyn is more important than a revolution in China.' Is there an equivalent for preachers?

Precise

It is not enough just to draw a general principle out of a passage ('you should be holy'). The general principle must be pointed to specific, concrete, everyday situations by asking 'How? Where?

When?' John the Baptist preached the necessity of fruit-bearing repentance, but then specified which exact fruit each specific group should bring forth (Luke 3:10-14). David Veerman put it this way:

Application is answering two questions: So what? And Now what? The first question asks, 'Why is this passage important to me?' The second asks, 'What should I do about it today?'[10]

Hearers must not be left to make the point to themselves. As Bridges noted:

We must not expect our hearers to apply to themselves such unpalatable truths. So unnatural is this habit of personal application, that most will fit the doctrine to anyone but themselves.[11]

Massilon, a famous French preacher, used to say, 'I don't want people leaving my church saying, "What a wonderful sermon — what a wonderful preacher." I want them to go out saying, "I will do something."'

Another effective way of giving sermons 'point' is by directing applications to one overall applicatory aim, rather than just a series of disconnected exhortations. Bryan Chapell argues that this should be done at the very end of a sermon:

The last sixty seconds are typically the most dynamic moments in excellent sermons. With these final words, a preacher marshals the thought and emotion of an entire message into an exhortation that makes all that has preceded clear and compelling. A conclusion is a sermon's destination. Ending contents are alive-packed with tension, drama, energy, and emotion.[12]

Proportionate

Application must be varied and balanced. Some preachers can condemn while preaching on, 'Comfort my people'. Others can comfort when preaching from, 'Flee the wrath that is to come!' Proportion is achieved not only by preaching from passages that will allow us varied applications, but also by applying the word in a varied way.

Just as Christ and his Apostles did, preachers must call sinners to behold both the goodness and the severity of God. Most preachers have a tendency, a bias, a pre-disposition that they need to be aware of and fight against at times. Some are great comforters and some are great disturbers. We should be both. As John Stott said,

> Every preacher needs to be both a Boanerges (having the courage to disturb) and a Barnabas (having the charity to console).[13]

Passion

We shall return to this subject in our final chapter, but I do want to underline the importance of passion in application. There is no part of the sermon that requires more of the preacher's emotional involvement. Dabney wrote:

> To produce volition, it is not enough that the understanding be convinced; affection must also be aroused.[14]

To do this, the preacher's own feelings must reflect the nature of the application. He needs to be solemn when warning; be warm when comforting; be confident when encouraging, etc. Dabney, again, said,

The preacher's soul should here show itself fired with the force of the truth which has been developed, and glowing both with light and heat. The quality of unction should suffuse the end of your discourse, and bathe the truth in evangelical emotion. But this emotion must be genuine and not assumed; it must be spiritual, the zeal of heavenly love, and not the carnal heat of the mental gymnastic… It must disclose itself spontaneously and unannounced, as the gushing of a fountain which will not be suppressed. What can give this glow except the indwelling of the Holy Ghost? You are thus led again to that great, ever-recurring deduction, the first qualification of the sacred orator, the grace of Christ.[15]

This is what Samuel Rutherford referred to when he spoke of the need to preach a 'felt Christ.'

CONCLUSION

And so I close this chapter with an appeal for more Christ-centred application. In a sense, this is the most important point in this chapter because only Christ-centred application will deliver us from mere moralizing and latent legalism.

What is Christ-centred application? Well, if we are preaching from biblical history, then we should show how that history prefigures and points to Christ, or how it eventually leads to him. If preaching from the Psalms, we should show how appropriate they are for worshipping Christ. If preaching from the Proverbs, we must show how Christ is the ultimate Wisdom of God. If preaching from the prophets, we must show how they predict Christ. If preaching from the law, we must show how it reveals our need of Christ. If preaching practical duties, we must show how to motivate obedience by love to Christ. If preaching Christ's words, we should show how they magnify the Christ who spoke them. If preaching on suffering, we should show how they bring us into fellowship with Christ's sufferings. If preaching duty, then we need to show how Christ forgives our many failings in the line of duty. If preaching about love, we must show the example of Christ. If preaching about sin, we must show Christ as the only Saviour from sin. Let all our application lead to the feet of Christ.

9. APPLICATION (2)

THE PRACTICE OF APPLICATION

In the previous chapter, we examined some of the principles of sermon application. Now we will consider the practice of sermon application. Specifically, we will look at twenty methods of sermon application — twenty ways in which Scripture may be used in a life-changing way. We will briefly explain each method, give an example from Scripture to justify each method, and then give a sermon example. The main point is to show scriptural support for each way of applying Scripture. If we can do that then we are justified in using that method of application. Each of these twenty methods fits the definition of application we gave in the previous chapter:

> Application is the process by which the unchanging principles of God's Word are brought into life-changing contact with people who live in an ever-changing world.

Declaration

'Christianity begins with a triumphant indicative,' said Gresham Machen.[1] The sermon should be an authoritative declaration of divinely inspired truths that replaces ignorance with truth, and establishes the faith of God's people. Authoritative declaration of the truth changes lectures into sermons, transforms the ignorant and prejudiced, and also establishes and confirms the faith of God's people. It is easy to forget that truth well preached is itself life-changing.

Scriptural example

In Acts 17:22ff, Paul preaches the knowledge of God to ignorant and prejudiced hearers. He announces and declares life-changing historical and theological facts.

Sermon example

A sermon on 'God is love' (1 John 4:8) benefits its hearers by replacing misunderstanding and misconceptions about God's love with clear and accurate knowledge of it, transforming them in the process.

Exclamation

Information is made more memorable and engaging when it is applied by way of exclamation. The preacher does not just state the truth but accompanies it with expressions of emotion. It was Spurgeon who said that the preacher should pepper his sermons with many 'Ohs...' and 'Ahs...' An exclamative phrase may also begin with 'What...' or 'How...' For example, 'What a great Saviour!' or 'How great God is!' An exclamative like 'Woe!' may also deprecate errors and those who spread them. Both the 'Ohs!' and the 'Woes!' appeal to the heart as well as the head.

Scriptural example

The Psalms are full of exclamation (Ps. 8:1, 9; 73:19; 104:24). After explaining the mysterious and awesome sovereignty of God, the Apostle exclaims, 'Oh, the depth of the riches both of the wisdom and knowledge of God! How unsearchable *are* His judgements and His ways past finding out!' (Rom. 11:33). Also, see Matthew 23 for Christ's sevenfold woes as he denounces the Pharisees.

Sermon example

When preaching on the beauty of Christ, instead of stating coldly, 'Christ is beautiful', the preacher movingly exclaimed: 'O, the beauty of Christ!' This applies the truth to the feelings and inflames the heart.

Interrogation

Having given the information, and invited the congregation to enjoy it, the preacher then challenges his hearers with questions about their own relation to these truths.

Scriptural example

Interrogation abounds in Romans. For example: 'You, therefore, who teach another, do you not teach yourself? You who preach that a man should not steal, do you steal?' (Rom. 2:21). Notice also Isaiah's use of rhetorical questions in Isaiah 40:12-14.

Sermon example

A preacher concluded a sermon on doing religious things only to be seen and applauded by men (Matt. 6:1-6), with a series of questions: 'Why do you come to church? To be seen of men, or to see God? Why do you pray? So that others will hear, or so that God will hear?'

Obligation

The preacher takes the truth and lays practical obligations on his congregation by giving them imperatives and commands that follow logically from the truth.

Scriptural example

In Exodus 20, God says that he redeemed Israel (vv. 1-2), therefore they should obey him (vv. 3-17). Paul concludes the substantially doctrinal part of Romans (chapters 1-11) with a number of imperatives in chapter 12.

Sermon example

A sermon on the lukewarm church of Laodicea (Rev. 3:16) was permeated with imperatives such as, 'Be zealous ... committed ... serious ... wholehearted ... single-minded...' etc.

We must not confuse morality, which is biblical and Christ-honouring, with moralism, which is Christ-less and unbiblical. Biblical morality promotes ethical change that is empowered by thankfulness for Christ's forgiveness and prayer for Christ's power. Moralism is simply legalism or pharisaism — it sets out God's requirements and requires obedience. It fails to point the believer to Christ as the reason, basis and power for this obedience. While we must shun moralism, we must promote morality and its Christ-centred basis.

Exhortation

Somewhat less confrontational than the imperative is the hortatory, 'Let us...' Exhortations portray the preacher as more sympathetic and involved.

Scriptural example

The apostle Paul addresses his fellow converted Jews in the letter to the Hebrews with a number of mutual exhortations. 'Let us therefore come boldly to the throne of grace...' (Heb. 4:16; cf. 4:1, 11; 6:1).

Sermon example

In a sermon on the condescension of Christ in his incarnation (Phil. 2:5-11), the preacher followed the Apostle's application with mutual exhortations to peace, unity and humility (2:3) in imitation of Christ (2:5).

Motivation

Sometimes the preacher may add to the five methods listed so far, the *motives* for information, exclamation, interrogation, obligation and exhortation. He can increase the likelihood of his hearers receiving the information, joining him in the exclamation, answering the interrogation, binding themselves to the obligation, and agreeing with the exhortation by giving scriptural motives for doing so.

Scriptural example

In 1 Corinthians 15:34 the Apostle commanded his hearers, 'Awake to righteousness, and do not sin...' and then adds this motivating reason, 'for some do not have the knowledge of God. I speak *this* to your shame.'

Sermon example

When informing his congregation about the deceitful and desperately wicked nature of the human heart (Jer. 17:9), the preacher motivated his hearers to listen and respond by explaining the vital importance of knowing our disease if we are ever to seek the right cure.

Imitation

The preacher may take Old Testament history as an example of how believers should or should not act in similar circumstances.

Scriptural example

After highlighting parts of Israel's history, Paul said to the Corinthians, 'Now these things became our examples, to the intent that we should not lust after evil things as they also lusted' (1 Cor. 10:6; cf. v. 11).

Sermon example

At least one lesson from David facing Goliath (1 Sam. 17) is that the Christian should confront the enemies of God and his people. But the motivation and power for this must also be given: 'the name of the Lord.'

Illustration

Sometimes the best way to apply a truth is by illustration or metaphor, by telling a story or painting a picture. If the story is powerful enough, it will apply the truth without having to make the obvious connections.

W. E. Sangster suggests using illustration to cement the concluding application of the sermon:

> The people are a little tired, maybe, from thirty minutes of serious thinking, and yet one cannot part from them without gathering it all up for its final reception into their believing hearts. Put it in an illustration. Hold up a picture that will both recapitulate and apply all that is in your mind. Having given the illustration, end. Make the illustration so good that it is utterly unnecessary to add more than a concluding sentence or two afterward — and be glad when it does not even require that.[2]

Scriptural example

When Jesus wanted to apply the teaching of 'Love your neighbour as yourself' he told the story of the 'Good Samaritan' (Luke 10:29-37).

Sermon example

When a preacher wanted to emphasize the importance of 'keeping the heart' (Prov. 4:23) he used the illustration of a computer's main chip, its Central Processing Unit, and how it impacts on everything else.

Quotation

A preacher may apply Scripture by showing the truth and its relevance from the sayings and writings of others. This may help to buttress and emphasize the lessons in the sermon. There are many examples of the biblical authors using previously written Scripture in this way. However, there are also examples of the biblical authors using secular writers to help apply the truth.

Scriptural example

Apart from frequently quoting Old Testament Scripture, Paul quoted one of the Greek poets to support one of his applications during his sermon in Athens (Acts 17:28).

Sermon example

A preacher found that quoting the words of Spurgeon or Lloyd-Jones to support his teaching made his listeners more likely to receive the teaching. Another used the words of famous non-Christians to show the despair and meaninglessness in even the most 'successful' worldly lives. Such quotes can have a dramatic impact on unconverted hearers.

Conversation

One of the best ways to get a congregation's attention is to set up a dialogue or conversation between two people. It may be a debate between the preacher and an opponent, or it may be between the preacher and a genuine seeker after the truth.

Scriptural example

In the book of Romans, Paul frequently set up dialogues between himself and an opponent in order to apply the truth (Rom. 3:1-9; 6:1-3).

Sermon example

In a sermon on creation (Gen. 1:1), a preacher applied the truth by carrying on an imaginary conversation between himself and an evolutionist, answering the evolutionist's questions and challenging him in return.

Condemnation

Once the truth is taught, it may often be necessary for distortions and denials of the truth to be highlighted and condemned.

Scriptural example

Most of Jude's epistle is an exposure and condemnation of false teachers in the Church of Christ.

Sermon example

A sermon on the once-for-all uniqueness and sufficiency of Christ's death (Heb. 10:14) was concluded with reference to the teaching of the Roman Catholic Church regarding the ongoing sacrifice of Christ in the Mass, which the preacher showed to be both blasphemous and dangerous doctrine.

Invitation

Having set Christ forth, the preacher must call sinners to him.

Scriptural example

In Psalm 2, the Psalmist concludes his description of the Messiah's ultimate victory over his foes with, 'Kiss the Son, lest He be angry, and you perish in the way...' (Ps. 2:12).

Sermon example

No sermon on Christ as the good shepherd (John 10:14) could conclude without the hearers being called upon to follow him and be fed by him.

Demonstration

Sometimes it is not enough for preachers to simply urge their hearers to do this or that. They must show how to do this or that.

Scriptural example

When the Ten Commandments are given in Exodus 20, the following chapters give a number of concrete examples of how to obey them.

Sermon example

A preacher who was urging his hearers to evangelize the lost on the basis of 'You shall be witnesses to Me' (Acts 1:8) spent a large part of his sermon on the practicalities of how to evangelize in specific situations.

Adoration

It should be natural for a preacher to feel adoration welling up within his heart as he preaches the truth. And, as his devotional spirit is excited, he may let out expressions of worship or even brief petitions heavenwards. Such spontaneous uses of the truth bring its reality and importance home to the hearers.

Scriptural example

In the Psalms, the writers often move from 'third-person' narratives about God to 'second-person' addresses of praise to God (Ps. 106:4, 47).

Sermon example

When preaching on the everlasting destruction of sinners, a preacher found himself frequently turning from his congregation to God and saying things like, 'Lord Jesus, you are merciful... Gracious Lord, save us all from hell...'

Admonition

The congregation may need to be rebuked or admonished, leading to confession.

Scriptural example

Isaiah 1-39 sets forth God as the only hope for Israel, and in the light of that repeatedly admonishes and rebukes the people for turning away from God to ungodly nations to be their saviour (Isa. 30).

Sermon example

Someone preaching on 'Do not love the world...' (1 John 2:15) rebuked his hearers' worldliness and led the congregation in confessing, 'Holy God, we have loved the world, we have copied the world, we have followed the world, we have admired the world... Turn us and we shall be turned.'

Consolation

There are times when a congregation needs comfort and encouragement with the truth.

Scriptural example

In Isaiah 40-66, Isaiah turns from rebuke to comfort. His prophecies assume Israel captive in Babylon, and he encourages them to put their trust in God and look forward to a restoration to their land (e.g. Isa. 40).

Sermon example

A sermon on the Lord's post-denial pursuit of Peter (John 21) was used by a preacher to encourage backsliders not to despair, but to return to an all-merciful and all-forgiving God.

Examination

When preaching on the internal marks of a true Christian, the preacher will impress on his hearers the need to examine their own hearts to discover whether they have these marks. He will perhaps describe how a true Christian thinks and feels in certain situations and then contrast this with unbelievers.

Scriptural example

In Luke 6:20-26 the Lord describes the blessed identifying marks of the true Christian, and then contrasts this with the characteristics of the unbeliever.

Sermon example

In a sermon on 'The joy of the LORD is your strength' (Neh. 8:10), a preacher distinguished the joy of the Christian from the joy of the non-Christian by examining the object of each joy, the nature of each joy, the duration of each joy, and the end of each joy. Hearers were encouraged to search their own hearts to see which joy was their 'strength' and to derive comfort upon discovery of true spiritual joy.

Reconciliation

One important part of sermon application is to reconcile the truth of the preaching passage with modern science, with human experience, or even with the rest of Scripture. Without this the truth may meet resistance and have no life-changing impact.

Scriptural example

In Romans 9, the Apostle shows that the doctrine of human responsibility is not incompatible with divine sovereignty (Rom. 9:19-23).

Sermon example

In a sermon on God's 'leaving of Hezekiah' (2 Chron. 32:31) a preacher showed how this was consistent with the promise that God will never leave nor forsake his people (Heb. 13:5). He showed how the leaving was not objective but subjective, not in fact but only in feeling.

Anticipation

Many Scriptures were clearly intended by God to anticipate Christ's person and work. Although they may have had a primary reference to Israel and its experiences, subsequent Scriptures show that they had a further and higher significance.

Scriptural example

Jonah's 'resurrection' through repentance held out hope for Israel that if they repented of their prejudicial nationalism, the nation too could anticipate 'resurrection'.

Sermon example

On the authority of Christ himself (Matt. 12:39-40), a preacher may use Jonah's 'resurrection' as an anticipatory sign of Christ's resurrection, and hence also that of believers (1 Cor. 15:12 ff.).

Modernization

The Bible addressed the problems of an ancient people in ancient times. The preacher therefore has to 'modernize' when preaching on many passages. He must find out what the people were like and then find out the reason for the message God gave them — what problem was being addressed, etc. Having done that, the preacher can then deduce a timeless principle for modern application.

Scriptural example

In Deuteronomy 25:4, Moses instructed the children of Israel to allow the ox that was treading the corn to eat of the corn as it does so. In 1 Corinthians 9:9 and 1 Timothy 5:18, the Apostle took the principle behind the verse — the one who labours should be supported by those his labours benefit — and used it to justify preachers of the gospel being supported by the givings of the people they minister to.

Sermon example

'Divers weights *are* an abomination to the LORD, and dishonest scales are not good' (Prov. 20:23). Although few Christians use balances and weights in their daily lives today, a preacher took this text, extracted the principle of fairness and justice in both buying and selling, and on the basis of it exhorted present-day Christians to honesty, fairness and truthfulness, both in business life and personal life.

CONCLUSION

There are many complicated books on preaching which make the process of application so convoluted that many preachers give up trying to apply the Word, or feel inhibited from applying it to its full extent. However, if God gives us scriptural warrant for our methods of application, it really does not matter what anyone else says in opposition. Let the Word of God free us to apply it with life-changing power to our hearers.

10. PRESENTATION

=== *PREACHING A SERMON* ===

The behind-the-scenes work is over, and now the sermon is brought out into the light of day. The preacher knows what to say, but how should he say it? What will help the presentation and delivery of God's Word? These are the questions we wish to address in this final chapter.

I'm assuming that all the previous steps of sermon preparation have been completed. No amount of speaking skills can make up for a lack of substance. However, even the best sermon material needs to be delivered in the best way possible to maximize effectiveness.

Purity

No amount of theological substance or oratorical skills will make up for a preacher's lack of personal holiness. This is true if the pastor obviously does not practise what he preaches. However, it is also true when the inconsistency is not so public — when there is secret and private sin. The spiritually discerning among God's people can detect when the preacher's life does not match his lips. They may not be able to put their finger on it, and they may not be able to put their instincts into words, but they will have an unease, a sense of something not quite right, which will fatally undermine much that the preacher says.

On the other hand, a holy life will impart moral authority and spiritual power to a preacher's words. He will have an unction from on high that will impress and influence even the hardest of hearers. Dabney said,

> The hearer's apprehension of their minister's character is a most important element in his power of persuasion... The pastor's character speaks more loudly than his tongue.[1]

Prayer

There is no secret behind powerful preaching — apart from secret prayer. The biggest mistake preachers can make is to think that they can learn to preach powerfully from books, from seminars, or from lectures on preaching. No, for preaching to be powerful it must be preceded by, accompanied with, and followed by prayer.

It is prayer that imparts reality to sermons — the reality of God, of sin, of judgement, of heaven and hell, and of eternity. Such reality transforms mere lectures, talks and Bible studies into living and life-changing sermons. This cannot be learned from books, manufactured, or imitated.

It is an awful feeling for a preacher to stand up to preach knowing that he has hardly prayed about the sermon; that he has spent too long on preparing the sermon and not enough on preparing himself. Few things drain the power from a sermon as much as prayerless preparation and delivery.

The preacher should spend at least thirty minutes in prayer with his completed sermon. He should go over each section, applying it to himself. If teaching a virtue, he should pray for that virtue in his own soul. If preaching on a sin, he should confess his own sins in that area. If teaching about the person of Christ, he should spend time praising Christ directly for this aspect of his character or personality. He should pray for the right spirit and manner for each section of the sermon. He might also pray for:

- Courage in sections where the fear of man might threaten;
- Specific people he wants to help with his sermon;
- The avoidance of misunderstanding;
- Help with timing and with complicated sections;
- The knowledge of what to leave out;
- The Spirit of God to give him extra thoughts and words that he had not prepared;
- Wisdom to know how to react to people's comments and responses.

The first thing a preacher should do when arriving home after preaching is to go apart and pray. Perhaps it will be a prayer of thanksgiving or confession. Maybe he will pray for humility or encouragement. He will certainly want to pray that the seed sown would be protected and watered and bring forth fruit. Patience and submission should also be prayed for. When a preacher has poured ten or even twenty hours into a sermon and then poured himself out in preaching it, it can be painfully frustrating when nothing seems to have been achieved. Instead of taking out these frustrations on family or on the congregation, they should be honestly brought to the Lord in prayer, asking for patient faith and patient submission to God's sovereignty.

Preachers should cultivate the practice of not only praying before and after preaching, but during it. After every main point, or perhaps even after every sub-point, the preacher should briefly pause and silently pray for God to bless what has just been said and to guide in what is yet to be said.

Personality

'Be yourself.' It sounds simple, but it can be a real struggle. Acting is so easy — and common. It is common for young preachers to act older than their years. It is common for old preachers to act like teenagers. It is common for many preachers to mimic others they admire.

However, it is part of the preacher's task to be what God has made them to be. Yes, improve talents. Yes, grow in knowledge. Yes, learn from others. Be the best 'you' you can be. But, 'Be yourself.'

The preacher should not rebel against how God has made and gifted him. God has fitted and suited him for a particular time, place and people. To try and be like someone or something else will only hinder his ministry.

The older writers on homiletics argued that preaching should be a person's natural form of speaking — only somewhat amplified. Insincerity and artificiality are enemies. The voice and gestures should be 'natural.' Phillip Brooks spoke on 'The Two Elements in Preaching', and gave this definition:

> Preaching is the communication of truth by man to men. It has in it two essential elements, truth and personality. Neither of those can it spare and still be preaching ... Preaching is the bringing of truth through personality ... The truth is in itself a fixed and stable element; the personality is a varying and growing element.[2]

Posture

One of the verses that the preacher should always keep before him is, 'We are ambassadors for Christ' (2 Cor. 5:20). On the one hand preachers are not ambassadors for earthly monarchs, with all the aloofness and detachment that implies. They are ambassadors of Christ, the one who ate and drank with publicans and sinners. Arrogance and pride do not fit ambassadors of the Servant-King.

On the other hand they are ambassadors, which implies a responsibility to represent their King accurately, and to communicate the serious message they have been given with dignity, sobriety, solemnity and fearlessness. They are not in the pulpit to have a casual, hands-in-pocket chat with some friends. Their clothing, posture, demeanour and expression all preach their own sermon and carry their own message into the hearts of our hearers.

Dabney counsels:

> Every tone, and look, and gesture, from the moment he enters the pulpit until he leaves it, the structure of every sentence in his sermon, should reveal a soul in which levity, self-seeking and vanity are annihilated by the absorbing sense of divine things.[3]

Facial expressions and bodily gestures should be allowed to flow and vary with the material and spirit of the words. Researchers have categorized over 500,000 different physical gestures. Body-language, therefore, has huge potential to underline or undermine your message. Common mistakes include being too tense or too casual, too energetic or too still, too nervous or too confident, repeating the same gesture again and again, fiddling with fingers or ring, swaying from side to side etc.

Pronunciation

The preacher has a number of God-given voice tools in his vocal toolbox.

Volume

There is no point in preaching if the sermon is not audible. The voice should be loud enough to be heard by all hearers throughout the whole sermon. Volume should flow naturally from the subject material and its impact on the preacher's heart. It should not be manufactured. Special care should be taken not to drop the volume at the end of sentences.

Diction

Diction — the clarity with which words are spoken — is actually more important than volume when it comes to our hearers. People will hear even the whispers of someone who clearly separates and articulates all the consonants and syllables of his words without slurring or mumbling. But without clear diction, all shouting is in vain.

Tone

Tone describes not so much the volume of the note but the pitch of it, from low to high. Just as in ordinary speech our voice moves through a range of tones, so they should in the pulpit also. Normally, sermons begin with a low tone and pitch, and these usually heighten as the sermon progresses to application. This is the main way to avoid monotony.

Emphasis

When we talk to people, we naturally emphasize what we most want our hearer to listen to. We do this by an increase in volume, diction, or tone for a word or two. This natural 'tool' for making one word or phrase stand out from the rest is an important and much underused vocal asset.

Pace

Another 'tool' is pace. Regular and appropriate variations in pace make listening easier. Care should be taken not to speak like a train — and also not to speak like a tortoise.

Wise insertion of appropriate pauses allows the truth to sink in and influence the heart before moving on to the next point.

A related issue is the length of a sermon. A preacher should only very rarely exceed the time granted. Preaching for less than the usual time is rare, but sometimes the message can be more effective if stopped early, the main point having been made. Too long a sermon will usually result in hearers going home with less rather than more.

If a preacher senses he is going overtime, it is usually better to cut out a section, rather than speak like a speeding train. The most common area for preachers to lose time is at the beginning.

Another possibility, usually quite rare, is for a preacher to run out of things to say when he still has some preaching time left. Perhaps not enough material was prepared. Or maybe too fast a pace pushed him through his material too quickly. The solution to this is very simple. Stop! Let me say that again. Stop! A preacher can destroy so much of the work he has already done if he simply starts ad-libbing or, even worse, starts repeating what he has already said. Very few people will complain if a sermon is shorter than expected.

Repetition

The theme and main points should be repeated as often as necessary to impress the structure and emphasis of the message. John MacArthur explains:

> As you move from one point to the next, use brief
> transitional sentences to review the points you have

already covered. Restate the central idea of the message as often as appropriate.[4]

Variety

Variety simply refers to the wise and judicious combination of these vocal tools. Just as when building a house, the preacher should wisely vary the use of his tools, moving from loud to quiet, from fast to slow, from didactic to emotional, etc. Dabney advises us:

> Take your model here from Nature. She does not thunder all the year; she gives us sunshine, gentle breezes, a sky chequered with lights and shades, the stiffening gale, and sometimes the rending storm. So no hearer can endure a tempest of rhetoric throughout the discourse.[5]

Passion

Professor John Murray once said, 'To me, preaching without passion, is not preaching at all.' A preacher cannot expect people to be moved and affected by truths that do not seem to move him. He must not only believe what he says, but feel it also. He must aim to be deeply affected by the truths he proclaims. Gardiner Spring said of the preacher,

> He must feel his subject. It is as marvelous as it is mournful, that the weighty and thrilling truths of God's Word lose so much of their force from the little interest the preacher himself feels in his theme... No preacher can sustain the attention of a people unless he feels his subject; nor can he long sustain it, unless he feels it deeply. If he would make others solemn, he himself must be solemn; he must have fellowship with the truths he utters. He must preach as though he were in sight of the cross, and heard the

groans of the Mighty Sufferer of Calvary; as though the judgement were set, and the books opened; as though the sentence were just about to be passed which decided the destinies of men; as though he had been looking into the pit of despair; as well as drawing aside the veil, and taking a view of the unutterable glory.[6]

This is not an argument for artificial emotion. Our emphasis throughout this chapter is on delivering sermons in a 'natural' way. When a house is on fire the passer-by does not spend any time thinking about how best to say the words 'Fire, fire!' The vocal sentiments and accompanying gestures will come spontaneously and automatically. So it should be with the preacher. If he feels the power of divine truth as he ought, his arms, body and voice will fit the words without too much conscious effort. Bridges and Alexander underline this:

Preaching is not the work of the lungs, or the mimicry of gesture, or the impulse of uncontrollable feeling; but the spiritual energy of a heart constrained by the love of Christ, and devoted to the care of those immortal souls for whom Christ died.[7]

Preaching should be with affectionate earnestness and tenderness. The appearance of coldness and indifference in the preacher to the awful and interesting truths of God's Word must have a most unhappy effect on the minds of the hearers... A man pleading for the life of another must not appear as one discoursing on an indifferent subject.[8]

People

That brings us on to 'people'. The preacher has one eye looking towards God, and another looking towards his congregation.

He looks to God and asks: 'What do you want me to say?' But he also looks at his people and asks: 'Are you listening to and understanding what God has given me to say?' As in ordinary conversation, we must maintain maximum eye-contact with our listeners if we want to convince people that we are talking to them. Eye-contact also helps the preacher to maintain sensitivity to the age, education, spiritual condition and responsiveness of the congregation. In connection with this, Martin Lloyd-Jones said,

> Another element to which I attach importance is that the preacher while speaking should in a sense be deriving something from his congregation. There are those present in the congregation who are spiritually-minded people, and filled with the Spirit, and they make their contribution to the occasion. There is always an element of exchange in true preaching.[9]

Thorough preparation and familiarity with the sermon material will free the preacher to engage empathetically with the hearers. The more familiar we are with the road, the more we will be able to take in the surroundings. Charles Bridges wrote:

> The sight of his people in the presence of God — their very countenances — their attention or listlessness — their feeding interest or apparent dislike — suggests many points of animated address, which did not occur in the study; excites many visible impressions, which awakens corresponding sympathy and interest in his congregation.[10]

Plainness

For many years we've rightly bemoaned the widespread blight of too many shallow sermons. And, of course, that problem remains a problem. However, in many circles, especially perhaps in some Reformed churches, we may be in danger of over-complicating sermons. By over-complicating sermons I mean:

- **Too much material:** Far too much content crammed into far too little space.
- **Too many words:** Just because someone can speak 200 words per minute without a breath, does not mean that we can hear and understand at that rate.
- **Too many long words:** Why use long words when there are perfectly adequate shorter substitutes? And why use any Latin/Greek/Hebrew words?
- **Too many long sentences:** Readers may be able to follow four-line sentences (and two line headings), but not hearers.
- **Too long arguments:** If it takes a preacher twenty minutes and twenty steps of logic to prove his point, he'll be proving it to himself alone.
- **Simply too long:** There is surely a happy medium between ten-minute sermon strolls and sixty-plus minute marathons.
- **Too many headings:** By the sixth sub-point of the fourth main point, I'm gone.
- **Too much logic, not enough likes:** Just read the Gospels and ask yourself if you are like picture-painting Jesus or philosophical Plato. Yes, we need logic. But we also need 'likes' (e.g. the kingdom of heaven is like...) and stories (e.g. there was a rich man...).
- **Too many quotations:** *The New Treasury of Scripture Knowledge* is a great servant but a wearisome master. Take your preaching text and dig deep into it until you strike fresh water, rather than leave it behind to dig hundreds of dry one-inch Scripture-reference holes all over the desert. And though we may love quotes from Pastor Puritan, Pastor Spurgeon, and Pastor Lloyd-Jones, we really came to hear Pastor You.

- **Too much clutter**: Is that paragraph/sentence necessary? I know it's nice, but is it necessary?
- **Too much reading**: If forced to speak without notes, or with only a one-page outline, preachers would have to simplify. Preaching from a full manuscript allows much more complex arguments and sentences to be used. If a preacher must write everything out in full, then he should write in an oral style to avoid sermons becoming lectures.
- **Too much doctrine**: Systematic theology is wonderful. Biblical theology is great. But simply explaining the text is better than both. Systematic and biblical theology help us to understand the text but they should not be imposed on a text. It may perhaps help us if we try to imagine explaining the text to a twelve-year-old, then a ten-year-old, then... But please, please, please just explain the text.

It is wonderful that many Reformed pulpits are being filled with well-studied and well-prepared sermons full of biblical truth. But I'm afraid that many of our hearers can't swallow the great chunks of red meat that are being served from some pulpits. Our hearers need meat, but they need it marinated, tenderized, well cooked, and even cut into mouth-size bites. Some even need help with chewing! (I'll stop there.)

There are two ways to uncomplicate sermons: the first is intellectual and the second is spiritual. The *intellectual solution* involves the strenuous mental power-lifting of ruthlessly simplifying every sermon. Any fool can preach like a genius, but it takes a genius to preach simply. And by genius, I don't mean that some people have an innate ability to make the profound simple. Genius is usually the end-result of extremely hard work. There is a massive difference (about ten hours' difference) between preparing simple sermons and preparing simplistic sermons.

Most of my sermons are preachable after about eight to ten hours of work. But if I want the maximum number of my hearers to have maximum understanding, I must tie myself to the desk and push my brain to prune, shorten, clarify, illustrate, etc., for at least another two hours. Apart from studying how some of the best preachers manage to communicate deep truth without drowning their hearers, the best resource I've come across is William Zinser's book *On Writing Well*. We would do well to read and re-read (and re-read) pages 7 to 23; and to give sustained study to pages 10 to 11 where Zinser takes a knife to a manuscript. We should then sharpen our own knives.

Old Princeton professor, J. W. Alexander, wrote:

It is an interesting observation that some of the greatest sermons are deceptively simple in design and development. Simplicity in design, organization and development is the mark of a great communicator. Complexity confounds — simplicity satisfies.

The *spiritual solution* is a love for souls. That old-fashioned phrase must become a modern-day reality in our pulpits. If we love our hearers and want to see them live better here, and also prepare for life hereafter, we will do everything to simplify our sermons for their benefit. If we keep the spiritual welfare and eternal destiny of our hearers in front of us at all times, making ourselves understood will become a life-or-death matter.

It is wonderful that God is calling preachers with huge brains into the ministry of the Word. But huge brains need huge hearts if they are to lovingly and sympathetically serve God's less gifted (but maybe more-graced?) children.

In *Truth Applied* Jay Adams relates how Martin Luther initially used churchy academic jargon when he preached to nuns in a convent chapel. But, when he became the pastor of the town church at Wittenberg, he realized that he had to work at making himself understood. He used children for his standard of intelligibility. 'I preach to little Hans and Elisabeth,' he said.

If they could understand, others could too. He refused to play up to the educated in his congregation. 'When I preach here at Wittenberg, I descend to the lowest level. I do not look at the doctors or masters, of whom about forty are present, but at the hundred or thousand young people. To them I preach... If the others do not want to listen — the door is open.'[11]

Every preacher should long to fit the description of Luther: 'It was impossible to misunderstand him.'

Paper

Our earlier emphasis on maintaining maximum eye-contact brings us on to sermon notes.

John Broadus identified four basic methods of delivery:

- **Reading:** The preacher takes his manuscript into the pulpit and reads from it;
- **Reciting:** The speaker repeats from memory what has been written and learned;
- **Extemporizing:** The plan of the discourse is drawn out on paper and all the principal points are stated or suggested, but the language is extemporaneous;
- **Freely delivering:** After thorough preparation, the preacher goes into the pulpit without notes or manuscript and without conscious effort to memorize the sermon.[12]

The method chosen will determine how much paper is brought into the pulpit. I do not want to set down rules about this as much will depend on the preacher and his hearers. However, if there is a danger in our days it is probably too much reliance upon notes. We are all aghast at the idea of someone going into a pulpit unprepared and just rambling around for a time. However, the Reformed Church is perhaps in danger of going to the other extreme, of having such over-prepared sermons that the amount of paper required to preach them is increasing more and more, as is reliance on the manuscript. We must also recognize that this age prefers to be spoken to personally and relationally. There is nothing more authentic than a man preaching eyeball to eyeball, heart to heart, without anything intervening.

We should always remember that while pulpit paper may contain what is to be communicated, it can also become one of the greatest barriers to communication. Often the preacher's eyes are more on this than on his congregation. Al Martin commented on this:

> The issue is not how much written composition is done in the study or how much written material is brought into the pulpit. The issue is how much dependence upon and preoccupation with written material is manifested in the act of preaching. To state the matter another way, the issue is how much mental and physical attachment is there to one's paper. At the end of the day we are not so much concerned with issues of paper and print, but with the issues of eyes and brains.[13]

Listen to these strong words from Dabney:

> Reading a manuscript to the people can never, with any justice, be termed preaching... In the delivery of the sermon there can be no exception in favor of the mere reader. How can he whose eyes are fixed upon the paper before him, who performs the mechanical task of reciting the very words inscribed upon it, have the inflections, the emphasis, the look, the gesture, the flexibility, the fire, or oratorical actions? Mere reading, then, should be sternly banished from the pulpit, except in those rare cases in which the didactic purpose supersedes the rhetorical, and exact verbal accuracy is more essential than eloquence.[14]

Shedd argued that young preachers should from the very beginning of their ministries preach at least one extemporaneous sermon every week. By this he did not mean preaching without study or preparation — quite the opposite. Extemporaneous sermons require more preparation in many ways. What he meant was reducing the sermon to one page of skeleton outline, and becoming so familiar with it, that referring to it during the act of preaching is minimized. He then encouraged the preacher to gradually reduce the size of the skeleton, and his dependence upon it. The ideas should be pre-arranged but exact expression of them left to the moment of preaching. Shedd gives these requirements for extemporaneous preaching:

- A heart glowing and beating with evangelical affections;
- A methodical intellect — to organize the sermon material into a clear and logical structure;
- The power of amplification — or the ability to expand upon a theme;
- A precise and accurate mode of expression;
- Patient and persevering practice.

To these we would add, prayerful dependence upon the Holy Spirit for each and all of these requirements.

I would also recommend the following to decrease reliance on paper in the pulpit.

Saturation

The preacher must be saturated in his material. This is one of the benefits of preparing nearer the time of sermon delivery. Then, not just the final thoughts but the actual thought processes will be much fresher in the mind. The longer the time period between preparation and preaching, the more the preacher will have to rely on his notes. I also find that praying over my notes, applying them to myself, really helps to embed the sermon in the heart as well as the head.

Scriptural

If the text is just a pretext for some topical sermon with little connection to the text, the preacher will be much more reliant on notes. But if the sermon points and material flow naturally out of Scripture, then that's a huge help to reducing reliance on notes. The text can provide the prompts.

Structure

Preaching without notes requires a clear structure for the sermon material. It is much easier to remember five bullet points than a five-line paragraph. Using the outlining feature of a Word processor and the same lettering/spacing standard each time will train the mind to step through the process.

Summarize

The points and sub-points should be summarized, and the words cut down more and more until the main points and sub-points are no more than three to five words, and explanatory sentences are no more than one line long. I would recommend ending with no more than one page of a summary.

Stress

On the one-page summary, the structure and the main word in each point and sentence should be stressed or highlighted. Again, using the same colours each time, a highlight marker can be used to colour the main points and sub-points. This will help 'photograph' the structure into the mind.

Then, using a dark pen, the key word in each point, sub-point and line can be underlined. This word should be one that 'triggers' memory of the whole point/line. The first letter of each point can be written in the left-hand margin. There will then be a series of letters running up and down the left side of the page. One main point letter, the sub-point letters, and the explanatory letters can then be memorized. Recalling the word and phrase or sentence related to each letter may need some practice. But the letter should trigger a word that triggers the point.

Study

This method does not advocate memorizing the sermon word for word. Instead it requires that the preacher have a good vocabulary available to draw on. He will need to stock his mind with words so that the trigger word will pull in suitable other words to speak. He should read widely and constantly in various kinds of literature, including a quality newspaper and recent biographies. This will keep vocabulary fresh, contemporary and less clichéd.

Start

The hardest step here is simply to start. It is like learning to swim for the first time without a flotation device, or learning to ride a bike without stabilizers. It is a large psychological barrier. So, let me give some helps to starting.

First, it is better to start small. Instead of launching out with a full sermon, a small section should be chosen, and a commitment made to preaching it without notes by following the procedure outlined above. Next time, a larger section or two sections can be attempted, and so on. The mind will get into a groove and confidence will grow.

Second, in case of a total 'blank', there should be a back-up plan in the form of some notes in a pocket or in the Bible. The great temptation here though is that, knowing the back-up plan, the mind will take the easiest path. If a preacher knows there is no lifebelt, he will prepare much better for the water!

Third, it is wise not to try to memorize Scripture references or quotations. These should be written down on a small paper so that they can be read. That will save a lot of mental work. Also, quotations tend to carry more authority if read rather than repeated from memory.

Presence

So much of what we have covered so far will fall into its own place if we cultivate a consciousness of preaching in the presence of God. This consciousness pervaded the apostle Paul's preaching: 'For we are not, as so many, peddling the word of God; but as of sincerity, but as from God, *we speak in the sight of God in Christ*' (2 Cor. 2:17). 'Again, do you think that we excuse ourselves to you? *We speak before God in Christ*. But *we do* all things, beloved, for your edification' (2 Cor. 12:19, italics mine).

As the best ambassador is the man who best knows the One who has sent him, the best place to learn how to communicate God's Word is in God's presence. He is the greatest communicator, and time spent with him will make preachers into more effective ambassadors for him.

This God-consciousness will also deal a hammer blow to all theatrics and hypocrisy, while cultivating dignity and seriousness. It will create humble minds and humble motives. We are the ministers of a great king, and are entrusted with an important embassy. Charles Bridges says,

> The most pernicious and debasing evil of all is, a convert-ing our sacred office into a medium for setting forth our own excellence — prostituting the glories of the cross for the indulgence of our own pride, drawing a veil over the

glories of our adorable Master and committing a robbery against him, even in the professed business to exalt him. This is to lose sight of the great end of the Ministry — commending ourselves, instead of our Master, to the regard of our people... Our business is to make men think, not of our eloquence, but of their own souls; to attend, not to our fine language, but to their own everlasting interest. Our duty is ... not to stroke the ear, but to strike the heart.[15]

A preacher cannot bear witness to Christ and to himself at the same time. He must aim to unveil Christ and conceal himself. His is to have the best-man attitude — doing all he can to facilitate the marriage of the bride to the bridegroom and doing nothing to come between them.

This awareness of God will also help preachers to react to comments after preaching. If someone praises the sermon, he redirects the attention to God by saying something like, 'God be thanked for his wonderful Word!' or 'Isn't the gospel of Christ so rich!' If someone criticizes the sermon, then perhaps he might say, 'Thank you for your comments. I will take them to the Lord and ask him to show me if I have erred in some ways. Do you want me to get back to you about this when I've thought and prayed about it?'

'Lo, I am with you' is both a comfort and a challenge. It is a comfort because effective preaching needs a three-sided encounter — the preacher, the hearer and God. It is one of the great preaching experiences when we begin to feel like spectators standing on the side watching God at work. It is a challenge because God is listening, watching and taking notes. And, one day, he will call to account.

NOTES

Chapter 1

1. J. W. Alexander, *Thoughts on Preaching* (Edinburgh: Banner of Truth, 1988), 9.
2. A. Martin, *Prepared to Preach* (Strathpine North, Covenanter Press, 1986), 27.
3. Alexander, 105.
4. Michael P. Barrett, *Beginning at Moses* (Greenville, SC: Ambassador-Emerald International, 2001), 5.
5. Although hermeneutics, the study of principles of interpretation, lie beyond the scope of this short book, a companion volume on that subject is in the pipeline.
6. Barrett, 5.
7. R. L. Dabney, *Lectures on Sacred Rhetoric* (Edinburgh: Banner of Truth, 1979), 261, 263.

Chapter 2

1. J. I. Packer, *The Preacher and Preaching* (NJ: P&R, 1986), 4.
2. *Ibid.*, 4.

3. J. Stott, *Between Two Worlds* (Grand Rapids, MI: Eerdmans, 1982), 126.
4. Dabney, 75.
5. Donald Coggan, *Stewards of Grace* (Hodder & Stoughton, 1958), 46.
6. W. G. T. Shedd, *Homiletics & Pastoral Theology* (London: Banner of Truth, 1965), 153-154.
7. C. H. Spurgeon, *Lectures to my Students* (London: Marshall, Morgan & Scott, 1965), 81.
8. S. Ferguson, *The Preacher and Preaching* (NJ: P&R, 1986), 196.
9. J. W. Alexander, *Thoughts on Preaching*, 24.
10. Spurgeon, 86.
11. Shedd, 153.
12. Ferguson, 197.
13. Spurgeon, 82.
14. Dabney, 97.

Chapter 3

1. J. E. Adams, 'Editorial: Good Preaching is Hard Work', *The Journal of Pastoral Practice* 4, no.2 (1980): 1.
2. W. E. Sangster, *The Craft of the Sermon* (Philadelphia, Westminster Press, 1960), 157.
3. D. Stuart, *Old Testament Exegesis* (Louisville: Westminster John Knox Press, 2001), Preface x.
4. Stuart, 1.
5. Cited in John MacArthur, *Rediscovering Expository Preaching* (Dallas: Word Publishing, 1992), 143.
6. Stuart, 75.
7. *Ibid.*, 75.
8. *Ibid.*,74.
9. S. Greidanus, *The Modern Preacher and the Ancient Text*

(Grand Rapids: Eerdmans, 2003), 107.
10. *Ibid.*, 110-111.
11. Stuart, 26.

Chapter 4

1. C. H. Spurgeon, *Lectures to my Students*, 70.
2. J. Broadus, *The Preparation and Delivery of Sermons* (New York: Doubleday, Doran & Co, 1929), 79.
3. *Ibid.*, 77.
4. *Ibid.*, 84.
5. Dabney, *Lectures on Sacred Rhetoric*, 58.
6. Broadus, 94.
7. Cited in MacArthur, *Rediscovering Expository Preaching*, 255.
8. D. M. Lloyd-Jones, *Preaching and Preachers* (Grand Rapids: Zondervan, 1974), 63.
9. Cited in James Garretson, *Princeton and Preaching* (Edinburgh: Banner of Truth, 2005), 173.
10. W. E. Sangster, *The Craft of the Sermon*, 74-75.

Chapter 5

1. Dabney, *Lectures on Sacred Rhetoric*, 141.
2. Cited in Garretson, *Princeton and Preaching*, 98.
3. W. E. Sangster, *The Craft of Sermon Construction* (Philadelphia: Westminster Press, 1951), 119.
4. Cited in MacArthur, *Rediscovering Expository Preaching*, 242.
5. Dabney, 144.
6. Sangster, 133.
7. *Ibid.*, 134-135.

Chapter 6

1. J. Stott, *Between Two Worlds* (Grand Rapids: Eerdmans, 1987), 229.
2. G. Knecht, *The Preacher and Preaching* (NJ: P&R, 1986), 275-276.
3. D. M. Lloyd-Jones, *Preaching and Preachers*, 207-8.
4. Cited in Garretson, *Princeton and Preaching*, 104.
5. J. Broadus, *The Preparation and Delivery of Sermons*, 278.
6. Dabney, *Lectures on Sacred Rhetoric*, 109.
7. Charles Simeon, *Christian Observer*, Dec. 1821.
8. J. H. Jowett, *The Preacher: His Life & Work* (NY: G H Doran, 1912), 133.
9. Cited in Garretson, 96.
10. Broadus, 292.
11. Cited in Garretson, 103.
12. Lloyd-Jones, 207.

Chapter 8

1. Jay Adams, *Truth Applied* (London: Wakeman Trust, 1990), 17.
2. Douglas Stuart, *Old Testament Exegesis* (Louisville: Westminster Press, 2001), 27-28.
3. John Calvin, *Sermons on the Epistles to Timothy and Titus* (Edinburgh: Banner of Truth, 1983), 2 Timothy 4:1-2.
4. Stuart, 28.
5. Adams, 39.
6. Charles Bridges, *The Christian Ministry* (Edinburgh: Banner of Truth, 1983), 275.
7. Adams, 119.
8. Adams, 22ff.
9. Bridges, 271.

10. David Veerman, 'Sermons: Apply Within', *Leadership* (Spring 1990), 121.
11. Bridges, 270.
12. Bryan Chapell, *Christ-centered Preaching* (Grand Rapids: Baker, 2005), 254.
13. J. Stott, *Between Two Worlds* (Grand Rapids: Eerdmans, 1987), 315.
14. Dabney, *Lectures on Sacred Rhetoric*, 234.
15. *Ibid.*, 176.

Chapter 9

1. J. Gresham Machen, *Christianity and Liberalism* (Grand Rapids: Eerdmans, 1977), 47.
2. Sangster, *The Craft of the Sermon*, 144-145.

Chapter 10

1. Dabney, *Lectures on Sacred Rhetoric*, 261.
2. J. Stott, *Between Two Worlds* (Grand Rapids: Eerdmans, 1987), 266.
3. Dabney, 267-268.
4. J. MacArthur, *Rediscovering Expository Preaching*, 325.
5. Dabney, 320.
6. Gardiner Spring, *The Power of the Pulpit* (Edinburgh: Banner of Truth, 1986), 131-132.
7. C. Bridges, *The Christian Ministry* (Edinburgh: Banner of Truth, 1983), 320.
8. A. Alexander, quoted in *Princeton and Preaching* (Edinburgh: Banner of Truth, 2005), 189-190.
9. D. M. Lloyd-Jones, *Preaching & Preachers* (Grand Rapids: Zondervan, 1971), 84.
10. Bridges, 286-287.
11. Jay Adams, *Truth Applied*, 109-110.

12. J. Broadus, 432ff.
13. A. Martin, *Pastoral Theology Outline/Pastor's Conference* (1996), 11-12.
14. Dabney, 328-9.
15. Bridges, 330.